STRAIGHT TALK

A FRESH LOOK AT 1 TIMOTHY

LEADER'S GUIDE

CRC Publications
Grand Rapids, Michigan

Acknowledgments

We are grateful to Paul Stoub for illustrating this book.

We are also grateful to Remkes Kooistra, retired pastor, who wrote the student text for this course.

 Printed in the United States of America on recycled paper. ♻
1-800-333-8300 (US); 1-800-263-4252 (CAN).

ISBN 1-56212-180-4

10 9 8 7 6 5 4 3 2 1

Contents

Introduction

A study of Paul's first letter to Timothy provides us with a fascinating window into one of the very first churches that sprang up in the Greek world. It offers much more than just historical appeal. The issues it deals with are as fresh and current today as they were when Paul first penned them. Had he mailed this letter to us directly, his advice would be no more meaningful and useful. As we work through the epistle chapter by chapter, we will go on a journey that will let us explore and discuss a wide variety of topics that are still very much alive in our own churches.

The textbook that accompanies this guide has been written by Dr. Remkes Kooistra, a minister-emeritus in the Christian Reformed Church. Dr. Kooistra lives in Waterloo, Ontario, Canada.

In its twelve chapters *Straight Talk* provides us with a biblical interpretation of many of 1 Timothy's key passages as well as suggestions for how they impact the issues they raise. Chapter 1 leads us to consider the question of authorship. Chapter 2 fills in much of the background and context of the letter by introducing us to its author and addressee. The remaining chapters walk us through the epistle, touching on matters ranging from false teachers to wine drinking. Throughout, Kooistra sprinkles examples that demonstrate how Paul's advice proved to be relevant and important in his own life. In that way we gain a sense of the historical dimension as well as the biblical one.

Kooistra's overarching perspective on 1 Timothy is that it constitutes Paul's attempt to anchor the Ephesian church firmly in the gospel that brought it into being. This can only happen if Paul can furnish them with solid leadership and sound structure. For this reason he has sent Timothy as an evangelist to provide the preaching, teaching, and administration that will consolidate the work Paul began among them. In this letter Paul provides Timothy with advice and regulations to build a sound administrative structure that will keep this church living and growing as God's family. These "house rules" form the foundations of a church order that will keep the church on track long after he and Timothy are both gone. When we apply these rules with sensitivity to our own culture and time, they still give excellent guidance for our church families.

The main objectives for this course are

- to provide participants with a framework for understanding 1 Timothy.
- to help them identify God's enduring will in Paul's specific exhortations.
- to determine how we, within our culture and time, are to live out God's will in the areas Paul raises.
- to evaluate how we are doing in meeting Paul's concerns for God's family and in envisioning how we can improve our Christian fellowship.

Using the Textbook

All group members should have a copy of the textbook *Straight Talk* by Remkes Kooistra. They should come to class prepared by reading the chapter that will be under discussion as well as the passage from Timothy with which it deals. Because these sessions are built on class participation and discussion, adequate preparation on their part is essential. The only exception to this is the first session, where opportunity will be given for participants to do their homework in class.

Leader's Role

This course emphasizes group participation and discussion. A typical session will be less like a formal, structured class and more like a group of adults meeting together for discussion. You and the others will be learning together.

You'll notice immediately that the sessions in this book contain more discussion suggestions than you'll be able to cover in a typical forty-five minute session. Our intent is not to frustrate you but to provide you with an abundance of material from which you can choose. This means that you'll be ignoring some of our questions. We also encourage you to change or replace questions and use your own approach to leading some of these sessions. In short, we hope you use this manual more as a resource than as a recipe.

Each session begins with "Introductory Comments and Background for the Leader," a section that will set the context and draw your attention to any unique problems in the session. It serves to guide your session preparation. That section is followed by "Purpose of the Study," which outlines and summarizes the goals and structure of the session. This section will also help as you prepare to lead each session. You can measure your success as leader, to some degree, by looking back over these purpose statements after leading a session, to determine how many of them you achieved together.

The main part of each session is divided into focus sections. Under each focus you will find suggestions, background commentary, and discussion questions. Use as many of the comments, questions, and ideas as seem appropriate for your group and your situation. Remember to encourage participants to bring their own questions and comments to each session too. Try to answer these questions together as you work toward understanding how Paul's straight talk to Timothy applies to us today.

The options at the end of each section suggest alternate approaches and ways of expanding each session. Unless you have an extra-long meeting time, using an option will mean leaving something out of the basic session plan. Again, you are the best judge of what will interest and meet the needs of your group.

Evaluation

As leader you will want to ask the group from time to time, "How are we doing?" Give people a chance to react to your use of group time and to the textbook. Is there anything they would like to do differently? Is there anything they would like repeated because it struck them as particularly meaningful or effective? Was anything left unresolved with which you still need to deal at greater length? Be candid and open with the group as you discuss how the sessions might be improved.

We would also be interested in hearing how your group is doing. We invite you to send your reactions, suggestions, or questions to

Straight Talk
Education Department
2850 Kalamazoo Avenue SE
Grand Rapids, MI 49560

SESSION ONE

Locating Timothy

Introductory and Background Comments for the Leader

In this first session your goal as leader is to let the group get its feet wet as comfortably as possible. The water's always chilly when we first plunge in: it takes time to develop rapport with one another, to get acquainted with the material, and to establish an enriching process. You'll need to apply some warm, friendly encouragement. The best way to do that is to show real interest in—even curiosity about—the participants as well as a genuine love for the biblical material under study. There's nothing wrong with "naming the demon" of boredom right up front. At first glance, as Kooistra readily admits, 1 Timothy is not the most exciting part of Scripture. But digging deeper, we soon lay bare the heart of the apostle to the Gentiles as it beats so tenderly in sync with that of our Great Shepherd for this fledgling flock. You may want to start informally. Chat with group members as they arrive so that you set a friendly tone that will remain throughout the course. Then you can ask members to introduce themselves and get their noses into the textbook in fairly short order. But always be sure to balance the personal concerns and experiences of the participants with the materials under study.

Participants may want to linger too long either on issues from the past or on the issues we face today. You'll want to keep them constantly relating the one to the other. Ideally the discussion will move beyond specific issues to explore how Paul reveals God's abiding will through them. That way participants will leave this course with more than some knowledge about 1 Timothy and the issues the church in Ephesus faced in those days. They will have a better idea of how to concretely interpret God's Word for our time.

Purpose of the Study

In this first session we will evaluate the commonly held opinion that Paul is the author of 1 Timothy. As Kooistra points out, this may seem self-evident to many of us, but it isn't.

We also will demonstrate why this issue is important. True, whether or not Paul actually wrote the letter does not make it any less the Word of God. But it significantly affects the way in which we understand the book. This issue allows us to examine a Reformed interpretation of Scripture that takes seriously the historical setting in which God first directed his Word to flesh and blood people in actual concrete situations.

Finally, we will survey a number of considerations surrounding the question of authorship so that we gain an idea of how such issues can be tackled. Our objective is not so much to have participants answer the question of authorship definitively in their own minds but to give them a sense of where we can go to find answers to this kind of question.

■ Focus 1: *Introductions*

Open the session by introducing yourself—giving some biographical details and sharing a bit of what you hope to get out of this course. Try to aim higher than "just surviving it!" It's important to create an atmosphere from the start where you learn *together*. If the class perceives that you are walking along with them on this journey of discovery, it will take a lot of heat off of you as leader because class members will not expect you to have all the answers.

Ask group participants to go around the circle and introduce themselves. Invite them to share what they hope to get out of the course. At the same time ask them to think of a church rule or procedure they find either really terrific or especially silly and to share that with the group. Explain that 1 Timothy deals a lot with church process, and it will be interesting to find out how our church order compares to that of the church of Ephesus.

After you've introduced yourselves, have the group list the major issues our church must tackle today. Ask someone to record suggestions on a poster board or blackboard for future reference. Keep it in view. As you get into 1 Timothy, your group may be surprised at the convergence of such issues over nineteen hundred years of church history. Point this out from time to time.

Finally, since you cannot assume that participants have read chapter one of *Straight Talk*, have them do so now.

■ Focus 2: *Ground Rules*

After allotting sufficient time for participants to read chapter one, alert them to the sad fact that this is the first and last time you will so generously grant them the luxury of doing their homework in class. From now on they should come prepared by reading each week's lesson at home. Emphasize how important it is that they do this—you are not here to lecture. Informed discussion is the engine that will drive this course.

Mention that you will keep these sessions informal, allowing lots of room for discussion and interaction. Assure them that you will consider their agenda as important as your own but that you will try to bring the discussion back on track if it wanders off too far or too long. Agree that it may be necessary at times to move on if some issues result in a stalemate. Your ultimate objective is not to reach consensus on every issue but to listen to each other and through that discussion to listen to what God has to say to us in 1 Timothy.

Finally, affirm your role as a discussion facilitator. Indicate that you will try to keep the discussions broadly based, inviting responses from the "still rivers" while respectfully moderating the "empty barrels."

■ Focus 3: *Tone*

Kooistra shares a wonderful description of the type of writing we find in 1 Timothy: "There are no fires, no torches here, but lamps, without strong flickering, useful for work in enclosed space." Ask group members to elaborate on what this might mean.

Kooistra uses the quote as a way of comparing 1 Timothy to other writings of Paul. He shows that 1 Timothy lacks the excitement of new ground being gained, as is true in earlier letters (where one would need to use campfires or torches that flare and flicker). Here the apostle sets guidelines for the ongoing, day-to-day life of the church as it must set up a routine (taking time to erect the steadier light of lamps).

■ Focus 4: *Who Cares?*

Because most of chapter one deals with the issue of authorship of 1 Timothy, it's important to raise two questions:

Q. May we even question what 1 Timothy 1:1 so clearly states—that Paul wrote it?

Kooistra argues that even if we have no reason or need to ask it for ourselves, we need to raise the question for those who do not share our convictions. The claim made in this verse could be made just as easily by an imposter. Kooistra advises us to go the long route and assume that if our belief holds water, we should be able to provide good, demonstrable reasons for it.

Whether group members or any skeptics they might meet would find the ones he gives convincing, you can discuss later. For now you only need to establish the fact that the question is legitimate. As Christians we need to give answers to questions we may not need to pose for ourselves: "Always be prepared to give an answer to everyone who asks you to give the reason for the hope that you have. But do this with gentleness and respect, keeping a clear conscience" (1 Pet. 3:15-16).

Q. So why does it matter if Paul wrote it or not?

A denial of Pauline authorship does not automatically lead us to conclude that 1 Timothy is not God's Word. We don't know the authors of many books in the Bible, and they are no less God's Word because of it.

The reason the question of authorship is important, however, is because the setting of a biblical book greatly affects the way we interpret it. When we try to find out what a Bible passage means to us today, we need to take into account what it meant to its original audience. The more we know about that context, the more clearly we understand the will of God reflected in it.

Dr. Gordon Spykman has provided a simple way of thinking about that. After letting the class kick the question around a bit, you may wish to propose his view.

Spykman observes that God's truth as revealed in Scripture always came in a specific form. It was addressed concretely to specific people in specific situations. Removed as we are by thousands of years of history, our situation is much different than that of biblical times. But the more we study the passage in its wider context, the more we gain an understanding of what God's norm, his abiding will, is as reflected in the way God spoke to that concrete situation. Having derived the norm, we can then apply that same norm to our particular situation and give it a new form to fit our day and age. We can diagram it as follows:

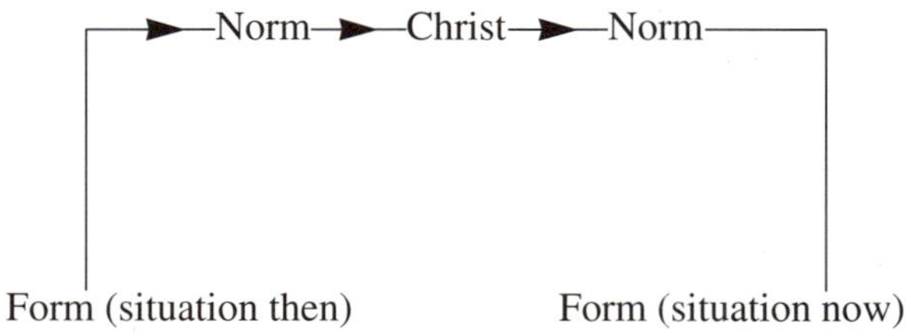

A simple example may help. Centuries ago, when our parents gave us an 8 p.m. bedtime, they did not intend for us to retain the *form* of that rule for the rest of our lives. Now that we're older, the *norm* remains the same: our parents still want us to get enough sleep. But we now must apply that norm to a brand-new situation. For forty-year-olds the old form of an 8 p.m. bedtime is no longer appropriate, unless we happen to be shift-workers or bakers. In the same way we who live in an age when Christ has come may not live in the old forms anymore; for example, we no longer follow the letter of the law of Moses. But in those old forms we still can discern the eternal will of God, which we should embody in New Testament forms today.

The upshot of this is that an imposter would have written 1 Timothy at a much later place and in very different circumstances than Paul would have. Taking into account such differences, we would interpret some passages very differently. Kooistra returns to this point a number of times throughout this study as he tries to help us fill in the details of the situation addressed. If Paul wrote this book, then we can accurately portray the false teachings he warns against. If some imposter wrote it, we have precious little to go on. If Paul wrote it, then we know that his plea for prayer for everyone came at a time of horrible persecution. If some imposter wrote it, the scene would be remarkably different. The same notion applies to 1 Timothy's discussion of overseers and widows.

You may ask the class to take a quick glance at the headings of 1 Timothy in their Bible and speculate on who else could have written it and under what circumstances. Don't expect to find agreement and don't take time to debate suggestions.

■ Focus 5: *Trivia Game*

Biblical trivia aren't trivial. Because our interpretation of Scripture is sensitive to actual historical situations, details can be very important. As a fun way to review some data, trivia questions can be one of the staples of this course. If you're game, divide the class into two groups by gender, age, geographical location, or whatever creates the greatest amount of friendly rivalry. Make it clear that these teams will be pitted against each other for the duration of the course and that you're playing for keeps: the losers must provide donuts for your last session. You should keep a running tally of the results, because adult education participants sometimes cheat and blame it on poor memory!

Ask the teams questions in turn. They may discuss their answer as a team, but they should go with the majority opinion. If they get the question wrong, the other team gets a turn to answer. As leader you can devise your own questions, of course, and substitute them for the ones included here.

Q. Who wrote Hebrews?

Nobody knows.

Q. Who wrote Job?

Nobody knows.

Q. How do we know Moses did not write the last part of the Pentateuch (the first five books of the Bible, traditionally attributed to him)?

It describes his death and what happened afterwards (Deut. 34).

Q. Was the gospel writer Luke an apostle?

No.

Q. Acts fills in for us much of the setting for 1 Timothy. To whom was it written? (No peeking!)

Theophilus.

Q. Into how many chapters was the original copy of 1 Timothy divided?

None. It was a letter. Text divisions were inserted many centuries later.

■ Focus 6: *Evaluating the Arguments*

After handing out suitable darts and laurels, ask the group to briefly summarize the four arguments Kooistra surveys that deal with the question of authorship of 1 Timothy. By all means let them refer to their text. Ask which of these they find persuasive. Next pose the bottom-line question:

Q. Did Paul write 1 Timothy?

Kooistra argues that he did. But allow for different opinions. Ask those who disagree with Kooistra to be sure to point out throughout the course where their point of view would make them disagree with Kooistra's interpretation of the letter.

Do try to get consensus on the fact that regardless of who wrote it, this letter is still God's Word to us. Inspiration does not depend on authorship. God can and did use all kinds of people to bring his Word. If anyone continues to dispute this point, then grant them the right to differ but assert the belief of the church universal that this letter is indeed "God-breathed."

End your discussion by summarizing the lesson. The question of authorship is important because it helps us to understand the context and setting of this letter. But it does not cast into doubt the fact that this is God's Word. The Holy Spirit clearly directed the process by which we have the Bible regardless of who wrote it.

■ Focus 7: *Closing*

Ask someone to read 2 Peter 1:16-21 as a fitting conclusion to the discussion.

Close the session with prayer. Invite prayer requests and then either close in prayer yourself, call on someone else to do so (having alerted them beforehand), or ask for sentence prayers. If you do the latter, be sure to specify who starts and who will close the prayer time. Also help the group to understand that quiet intervals need not embarrass us; they give us a time for our own silent prayers.

Adjourn by breathing threats of murderous vengeance upon all those who dare show up for the next session minus their Bibles, textbooks, and a firm grasp of the contents of chapter 2. Do append a personal benediction.

Options

Option 1: A Debatable Issue

After they have read chapter one, divide the class into two groups for a debate. Challenge group 1 to defend the proposition that Paul wrote 1 Timothy. Invite group 2 to oppose this position. Ask both groups to suspend their own personal judgment on the matter until both sides have been fairly presented. List the pro and con arguments they advance and review them for the class when you feel it's time to wrap things up. Ask each person what conclusion, if any, they themselves have reached.

Option 2: Pastoral Letters

After reading chapter one, distribute pens and paper. Ask each person to pretend to be the apostle Paul and write a letter to the pastor of your church. Tell them to include particular areas of concern about your congregation that you, the apostle, would definitely want to address. These may be specific, but remind the group that their letter will be circulated through the other churches of classis as well, so they should keep personalities out of it. Ask participants to share with the rest of the class these third, fourth, and fifth epistles of Paul to his nineteen-hundred-years-younger pastoral coworkers.

SESSION TWO

Meet Paul and Timothy

Introductory and Background Comments for the Leader

Our last session focused on the question of who wrote 1 Timothy. We explored the importance of this issue for our understanding of the actual historical setting in which this letter was written. The authorship of the book has many important implications for the way we interpret 1 Timothy. Kooistra helped us evaluate arguments for and against Pauline authorship and concluded that the apostle Paul was indeed the letter's author, and Timothy its recipient. That notion allows us to color in some of the picture, because both Acts and Paul's other letters tell us much about the prime participants and the churches they served.

In this chapter Kooistra sketches the lives of Paul and Timothy as we know them from the New Testament. Because the Bible leaves many gaps in our understanding, we rely on the testimony of early church historians as well. We sometimes need to take these sources with a grain of salt because they are often not as accurate or reliable as the biblical record.

Because this lesson is largely informational in content, it will be important to focus on the general themes that link together the material Kooistra presents. We do not want to get lost in the details. As much as possible we want to get a sense of who Paul and Timothy are and what their world looks like. The more we can reconstruct the feel of life in an emerging church surrounded by a hostile world, the more we can identify with Paul and Timothy.

We especially want to focus on the way in which we can see a higher hand at work in the lives of these two important church builders. Jesus came in "the fullness of time." God so guided events that the good news of his life, death, and resurrection burst into the world and reshaped it forever. It was providence that also supplied the emerging church with these two key players—Paul and Timothy. Their lives were designer-made. God fit them to the roles to which he called them.

Purpose of the Study

In this lesson we should not try to reconstruct the lives of Paul and Timothy so that we can fit all the pieces into one tidy biography. As Kooistra points out, the Bible does not provide us with enough information to develop a really satisfying time line. And it certainly does not allow us to tie up all the loose ends.

The real purpose of this lesson is to furnish us with enough of a picture of the lives of Paul and Timothy to help us understand the letter. So be sure to steer the discussion in that direction, not allowing the class to get too bogged down in all the historical complexities. Although some people find those interesting, they will not serve the major objective of gaining sufficient knowledge of the key players to understand why Paul writes what he writes to the young evangelist.

The more we get to know people, the more we care about them. This is certainly the case here. The clearer our picture of these men, the more closely we will identify with their challenges, their concerns, their hopes, their fears, and especially their faith, which overflows into such remarkably fruitful ministry. As servants of God called to a critically important task, they inspire us to look again at our own place in God's exciting, ongoing, Spirit-driven mission to reconcile the world to himself.

■ Focus 1: *Meetings*

Open the session with prayer, praising God for the way he uses diverse people and circumstances to bring about his kingdom. Ask for the Holy Spirit's presence as you reflect on the lives of Paul and Timothy so that you may discover the imprint of God's presence in their ministry.

Ask someone to read aloud 1 Corinthians 1:10-18. Discuss briefly this question:

Q. What does Paul identify as his central task in fulfilling God's mission?

Paul clearly states that his task is "to preach the gospel" (v. 17). However weakly he may proclaim it, the message of the cross reveals God's saving power to those who believe. Paul's whole life revolves around that ministry: his early years of preparation, his conversion, his missionary journeys with their hardships and perils, even his imprisonment and subsequent execution. That one task of spreading the good news picks up all the strands of his fascinating, complicated existence.

Ask someone else to read 1 Timothy 4:9-14. Discuss this question:

Q. What does Paul see as Timothy's mission?

These verses point out that Timothy's mission is also to preach and teach the word. He approaches this task with a very different background from Paul's. Yet his life, too, in a very different way, has brought him to this task.

■ Focus 2: *Lifelines*

Divide the class into two teams. Ask team A to take twenty minutes to read through Kooistra's account of Paul's life. Have members plot a rough event line on a large sheet of poster paper, including Kooistra's "guesstimates" of possible dates of significant events. Have group B do the same for Timothy's life. The lines should include the following data, although dates are only rough guesses:

Event Line for Paul:

- A.D. 05—born in Tarsis, Asia Minor; Jewish parents; Hellenistic culture; Roman citizenship
- A.D. 05—circumcised on the eighth day
- A.D. ??—as a young man educated by Rabbi Gamaliel
- A.D. ??—attends execution of Stephen
- A.D. ??—persecutes Christians
- A.D. ??—conversion on the road to Damascus
- A.D. ??—studies for thirteen years
- A.D. ??—sent out from Antioch on first missionary journey to Asia Minor
- A.D. ??—next two missionary journeys to Asia Minor, Macedonia, and Greece; suffers incredible hardships (2 Corinthians 11:23-28)
- A.D. ??—Jews attack Paul in Corinth (anchor date)
- A.D. ??—in custody in Jerusalem, Paul appeals to Caesar
- A.D. ??—imprisoned in Rome for two years
- A.D. ??—travels west as far as Spain
- A.D. 67—executed in Rome

Event Line for Timothy:

- A.D. ??—born in Lystra, Asia Minor; Jewish mother, Greek father
- A.D. ??—converted perhaps during Paul's first visit to Lystra
- A.D. ??—ordained as Paul's assistant
- A.D. ??—circumcised by Paul
- A.D. ??—joins Paul on second missionary journey
- A.D. ??—avoids imprisonment at Philippi
- A.D. ??—stays behind in Berea
- A.D. ??—rejoins Paul in Athens
- A.D. ??—travels to Thessalonica
- A.D. ??—rejoins Paul in Corinth

- A.D. ??— coauthors and possibly delivers Paul's first letter to the Thessalonians
- A.D. 53—joins Paul on third missionary journey; often accompanies him until A.D. 62
- A.D. 67—imprisoned with Paul in Rome but subsequently released
- A.D. ??— becomes first bishop of Ephesus
- A.D. ??— dies during riot in Ephesus

Once you have reconvened the group, compare the two lines and discuss ways in which the significant events of their lives contributed to Paul and Timothy's ability to fulfill their task. Write them on the board or a poster board. Here are some points you may want to include if they do not emerge from the group:

Pluses for Paul:

- Devout parents teach him God's covenant ways.
- His hometown acquaints him with how the world lives.
- Gamaliel's teaching gives him a good grounding in Scripture.
- His persecution of Christians keeps him humble after his conversion and always mindful of God's incredible forgiveness.
- His conversion leads him to Christ.
- His studies prepare him for his apostolic task.
- His hardships temper his resolve and prove his sincerity to those he evangelizes and pastors.
- Attacks by Jews steer Paul to spend more effort on evangelizing Gentiles.
- His arrest and appeal to Caesar allow him to publicly testify to his Lord before the authorities.
- His travel to Rome allows him to bring the gospel to the heart of the Roman Empire.
- His death, along with that of the other martyrs, draws many to the faith. As one early church historian put it, "The blood of the martyrs is the seed of the church."

Pluses for Timothy:

- Being born to a Jewish mother acquaints him with the Scriptures.
- His Greek father would make him conversant with that world as well.
- His conversion leads him to recognize Christ's lordship over his life.
- His ordination confirms his calling as an evangelist and pastor.
- His circumcision removes a significant barrier in his ministry to Jews.
- His travels with Paul allow him to assist in the work of spreading the gospel; his travels away from the apostle allow him to consolidate the work in emerging churches that need his pastoring.
- His imprisonment allows him to demonstrate his sincerity and commitment to the faith he proclaims.
- His appointment to the role of bishop allows him to extend his leadership to more than one congregation during a time when the church seeks a wider structure.

God provided Paul and Timothy with the gifts, circumstances, and opportunities to fulfill their ministry. Does God do that in our lives? Allow some open-ended discussion on this point.

■ Focus 3: *Personality Traits*

Using Kooistra's description and your group's own knowledge of Paul and Timothy, build a personality profile of each of them. Place their names on the board and ask the group to suggest words that identify and characterize these men.

Some descriptors to include for Paul: worldly-wise, godly, educated, dedicated, Pharisee, radical, penitent, believing, zealous, studious, courageous, bold, self-sacrificing, caring, persistent, humble, long-suffering, forceful, inspiring, thankful, faithful, and loving.

Words that may describe Timothy: believer, dedicated, committed, leader, helpful, pastoral, youthful, timid, fretful.

The following questions may be helpful to evaluate Paul and Timothy's suitability for their God-given tasks:

Q. What kind of work would you recommend to Paul and Timothy respectively if they came to you for career counseling?

Leave this discussion open-ended. If the group only responds that they would suggest missionary-pastor for both Paul and Timothy, press them to consider some alternatives as well. The exercise intends to stimulate the group to gather the descriptors into a useable image. You need not try to get the group to agree on any specific vocation.

Q. Were they suited to the task God gave them?

Again, allow group members some latitude on their responses. The record, however, shows that Paul and Timothy were indeed well-suited for their task. God knows his own.

■ Focus 4: *Trivia Game*

Time to renew hostilities. Divide the group into the battle groups established last session. If you have new combatants, divvy them up between the groups. Put last week's score on the board because we're shooting for the cumulative result. Then let the group fire away at the following questions. Remember, donuts are at stake! If you need to refresh your memory on how this exercise works, please refer to lesson 1, focus 5.

Q. Kooistra tells us that the name "Paul" means "short." What does "Timothy" mean?

"Timothy" means "honored of God."

Q. The phrase "Hellenistic culture" is used to describe the society in which Paul was raised. What does the word *Hellenistic* mean?

Greek. It refers to the culture spread through Asia Minor and beyond as a result of Greek domination of the near east under Alexander the Great and his cronies.

Q. Paul is sent out from Antioch. Name the country in which this city was located *at that time*.

Syria.

Q. Paul is an apostle. What does that term mean literally?

"One sent forth," or "sent out one."

Q. What was the disagreement that made Barnabas and Paul go their separate ways?

Barnabas wanted to take Mark along to revisit the churches they had begun. Paul would have none of it because Mark had deserted them on their previous journey (Acts 15:36-41). This paved the way for Timothy to join the team.

Q. How do we know that Timothy had a hand in writing 2 Corinthians?

2 Corinthians 1:1 tells us that clearly.

Tally up the score, add it to last week's, and save the results for next week's onslaught.

■ Focus 5: *Loose Ends*

Kooistra raises some interesting knots in the narrative of Paul and Timothy's life that will make for some good discussion. These will help fill out the picture we have of the apostle and the evangelist. Allow for some open-ended discussion on the following questions. It is not essential you deal with both of them, nor is it necessary to keep the discussion narrowly confined to the problems raised. Allow lots of latitude, and if the discussion wanders off topic, this is a good time to let the class go for it. Use these questions to round out the time remaining but allow for enough time to finish your session with the next focus point. Didn't get through them? No sweat! Kooistra already has.

You can refer the class back to the book.

Q. How can Paul say "[Jesus] considered me faithful, appointing me to his service" (1 Tim. 1:12), but in the same breath call himself "a blasphemer . . . the worst of sinners" (1 Tim. 1:13, 15)?

Kooistra points out that these words are sandwiched between Paul's observations that it was God's strength and grace that brought him to the point of being able to show faithfulness. His faithfulness was not a preexisting condition for God choosing him. Just the opposite: God's choosing of Paul makes him faithful enough to be considered a worthy candidate for the appointment to this service.

Q. In Matthew 23:9 our Lord warns, "Do not call anyone on earth 'father,' for you have one Father, and he is in heaven." How does that square with Paul calling Timothy his "true son" in 1 Timothy 1:2 and his "dear son" in 2 Timothy 1:2?

Paul is not denying the overarching fatherhood of God or placing himself in competition with God's claim on us. He simply recognizes the fact that through his teaching Timothy was included in God's family and groomed to take on his important ministry.

■ Focus 6: *Closing*

Ask the group to come prepared for the next session by reading lesson 3. Remind them to bring their Bibles, a notepad, and a pen or pencil.

Conclude the session by asking someone to read Hebrews 12:1-3. Comment on the "cloud of witnesses," including Paul and Timothy, who endured so much to bring the gospel to us. They now are watching what we do with our calling.

In closing prayer thank God for the great gifts he gave to the church and to us in the persons of Paul and Timothy. Ask that we, in turn, may also be faithful to our calling, in good times and bad.

Options

Option 1: Accurate Self-knowledge?

Divide the class into two groups, one answering the following question with respect to Timothy; the other, with respect to Paul:

Q. In comparing what Scripture tells you about this person to what he thinks about himself, how accurate is his self-image?

There are no hard and fast answers here. Your task in helping class members evaluate their responses is to pick up and emphasize the characteristics of Paul and Timothy that they bring out. List these on the board.

Q. How accurate is your self-image? How can you make it more so?

Accept various responses but be careful; this is sensitive ground for many people. Encourage people to state their true feelings, but do not force people to speak if they do not wish to do so. Two ways you can offer to allow people to gain a more realistic view of themselves is to compare what we think of ourselves to what the Bible says of us (see Ps. 139, Eph. 2:1-10, Rom. 8) and to develop relationships with fellow Christians in which we can receive honest feedback. The group may have other helpful suggestions.

Option 2: Video

Show a video on Paul's life. TRAVARCA, the audiovisual library of the Christian Reformed Church and the Reformed Church in America, has a series on Paul entitled "Discovering Paul." It offers twelve separate 20-25 minute sessions covering various aspects of Paul's life, each of which will stand well on its own. For more information contact TRAVARCA toll-free from the U.S. or Canada at 1-800-968-7221.

SESSION THREE

Heresy

Introductory and Background Comments for the Leader

1 Timothy 1

The last two sessions provided an introduction to our study of 1 Timothy. Session One led us to examine the issue of authorship and concluded that this letter was indeed written by the apostle Paul to his coworker Timothy. In Session Two we gained a greater understanding of Paul and Timothy as we surveyed the New Testament for information about them and filled in some blank spots with data provided by early church historians.

In this session we wade into the epistle itself. After a brief introduction Paul wastes no time in getting around to his dire warning against false teachings that threaten to pervert the truth of the gospel. The churches that have sprung up in response to the Word of God must remain ever vigilant. The power of evil is so strong that it can rob us of salvation by simply twisting God's truth into an abominable lie. Heresy that corrupts the truth from within remains one of the church's greatest enemies. In Ephesus it had already begun to rear its ugly head.

The issues raised in this chapter are not simply academic. Many modern heresies follow directly in the tracks of these earlier ones. Church members who have been lured into a prolonged discussion with followers of a sect or cult will immediately recognize the queasy feeling of knowing something's wrong, without knowing exactly where the expressed views have left the biblical track. Be sure to allow enough time for discussing modern heresies and how we can best combat them. Emphasize also that heresy is not only a matter of teaching but also of practice. Often we say the right thing, but our actions betray our denial of that confession.

For this session, as well as all future sessions, it will be important for participants to refer constantly to the passage under discussion. Ask them to bring their Bibles. And keep a few extras on hand for new members and for those whose weakness of mind makes them show up without one. Although husband and wife are one, ask them to take separate Bibles because they will want to refer to them often.

It is not necessary for all participants to have the same version of the Bible. In fact it will be good to have a variety, allowing participants to contribute and compare different translations. Take the opportunity to point out that Paul wrote his letter to Timothy in ancient Greek. Translations are at best approximations of actual meanings. This fact does not violate our trust in the authority of Scripture; it only points out that translations are human work and therefore fallible, incomplete, and transitory.

We will need to be watchful as we seek to understand the real meaning of the text. When we run stuck, we'll need to consult with resources that can tell us what the actual Greek text says. Kooistra does that for us on many occasions. If you wish, you can provide some worthwhile Bible tools for the class: a Bible dictionary, commentaries, a concordance, a Bible handbook. Your pastor or church librarian will be able to equip you with these items.

Purpose of the Study

The purpose of this lesson is to show us how to identify and deal with heresy—false teachings that can pervert our faith. We learn from the first chapter of 1 Timothy that heresy is not a new phenomenon and that even the New Testament church has suffered its onslaughts from infancy. They faced the same questions we face: How can an emerging church keep itself on track? How can it be sure that it remains faithful to the truth?

Some members of your group may feel that heresy is a remote issue without much practical value for us today. It may be true that within the church serious doctrinal deviations have become rare. But the next time their doorbell rings, and they are confronted with a pamphlet-toting canvasser of souls, they may change their tune. And when the doctrines to which we so readily assent seem to have no bearing on our daily walk with the Lord, all of us can become susceptible to a heretical virus. That's the most dangerous situation of all because we will follow the heresy unwittingly.

By paying careful attention to the way in which Paul identifies and deals with the heresies plaguing the Ephesians, we will be sensitized to similar heresies threatening us as well. And we will learn how to deal with them, constantly checking our beliefs in the light of the gospel. That is no mere theoretical exercise. God calls us daily to practice what we preach.

■ Focus 1: *Keeping the Faith*

Open the session with prayer, praising God for the greatness of his revelation. Give thanks for the gospel God has given us and ask for the presence of the Holy Spirit in this meeting so that you together may clearly understand it. Seek God's guidance in dealing with falsehoods that threaten our faith. Pray for love, patience, courage, and wisdom in dealing with those who are influenced by or trapped in heretical sects.

■ Focus 2: *Good Divisions and Bad*

Have a volunteer read 1 Timothy 1. Ask participants to follow along in their Bibles and point out any interesting variations in the version of the Bible they are reading. Summarize the observations on translations from the Background section above.

Note, as Kooistra points out, that not all divisions among people are bad. A large corporation cannot do business without breaking its workforce up into discreet departments. A world-embracing church must do the same thing. It should allow the numerous cells of the body of Christ to differentiate themselves into organs that bring their own unique contribution to the good of the whole.

Bad divisions occur when subgroups begin to take on lives of their own, rejecting the overarching beliefs, values, and mission to which they are called to contribute. When that happens within the body of Christ, then we speak of a sect or a cult.

Discuss the following question with your group:

Q. What are some sects or cults that have sprung up out of the Christian faith but have deviated from it to such an extent that they are generally no longer considered part of it?

Your list might include the following: Jehovah's Witnesses, Mormons, Moonies, Scientologists, Unitarians, theologically liberal congregations, Jonestown victims, and many others.

■ Focus 3: *Naming the Demons* (1:3-4)

Remind the class that Paul targets false doctrines, myths, and genealogies, which embroiled believers in endless controversies. He indicates that some of these teachings actually distorted the gospel while others distracted people from its real message.

Split the class into three groups. Ask group 1 to take a few minutes to list false modern-day teachings that are passed off as biblical teaching. One example you can suggest might be the notion that God will find you acceptable just because you tried to keep your nose clean.

Ask group 2 to list some modern-day myths that distract us from doing what is important by making us focus unduly on what is not. You might give them the example of the old adage "cleanliness is next to godliness."

Ask group 3 to respond to the issue Kooistra raises about Mormon beliefs concerning genealogies. Have them evaluate that belief as well as the value of tracing one's family roots in general. Reconvene the groups and ask them to report in turn. Allow questions, objections, and further suggestions from the group as you jot their responses on the board.

Some possible responses from group 1 might include the following:

- Jesus is the first creature, but he is not God (Jehovah's Witnesses).
- Jesus did not rise bodily from the dead (Jehovah's Witnesses).
- Like Adam we too can become gods (Mormons).
- God was once a human being who became as he is through dedicated effort (Mormons).
- Physical illness is an illusion caused by a lack of faith (Christian Science).
- It's good to pray to saints (Roman Catholicism).
- Jesus only saves us by setting a good example, not by paying for our sins (Christian humanism).
- Resurrections do not happen, so the story of the empty tomb is a pious fraud (Christian liberalism).

Possible responses from group 2 might include the following:

- Happiness is a good-looking body.
- The person who dies owning the most toys wins.
- Might makes right.
- Winning isn't everything, it's the *only* thing.
- You haven't lived until you've golfed.

- Striving for personal gain benefits the common good.
- When you have your health, you have everything.

Group 3 should take issue with the Mormon teaching that we can incorporate our ancestors into God's kingdom through baptisms for the dead. The Bible clearly teaches that salvation is a precious gift of God to those who believe (John 3:16-18). Mormons reject the witness of the church from the middle ages until the "true gospel" was once again revealed to Joseph Smith. It's the only way during those centuries that people had any hope for salvation. This idea conflicts with the confession of the church universal that God has never left himself without witnesses in the world. Although the church's proclamation suffered many distortions, it continued to point people to Jesus—"the way, the truth, and the life."

Allow some discussion on the merits of chasing down one's family tree. It provides a good hobby, but it has its pitfalls such as pride, fatalism, chauvinism, and an overindulgence in matters of family identity. Like any hobby it can take too much time and energy, and it may feed an overinflated ego. It makes no difference to God who your ancestors are. In this day and age God counts as children of Abraham those, and only those, who believe in his Son. Only that family tree, reshaped by God himself, matters.

■ Focus 4: *God's Economy* (1:4-11)

Provide a transition to Paul's discussion concerning the law of God by stating that the heretics of old are no different than those of today. They want to tell us how to live (1:7). They claim to know what God wants us to do, but they are wrong. Paul reminds us that God's law is good. It warns against those who pervert the freedom the gospel grants us. But the legalistic demands of a Jim Jones or a David Koresh or a Dr. Moon serve no useful purpose, and we should not allow ourselves to be bound by them. Instead, Paul tells us that we should do "God's work—which is by faith" (v. 4). Remind the class what Kooistra writes about this: "God's economy . . . rests in the faith spelled out in the Bible, containing as its most precious jewel the assurance that we are saved not by works but only by God's grace" (Eph. 2:8).

Return to the lists of focus 3. Raise the following question:

Q. What do the teachings you listed there demand from you that the Bible does not?

Your group will have its own answers. Here are some possible ones that may be representative:

- Jehovah's Witnesses demand a great deal of "kingdom service" to get one into heaven.
- Mormons demand a life of exemplary service to allow one to become divine.
- Christian Scientists demand heroic acts of faith to make people deny their physical ailments and to discourage them from seeking medical help.
- Christian humanists demand that we must follow Christ's example explicitly; there is no salvation unless we do.
- The body-shaping doctrine demands that we diet and exercise till we drop.
- The materialist myth makes us earn, earn, earn, and buy, buy, buy.
- Pragmatism demands that we succeed; failure is not acceptable.
- Golf, like any hobby, can easily demand too much of our time, money, and energy.
- Health nuts put us on strict regimens that make us pay undue attention to our bodies and not enough to what they are for.

■ Focus 5: *Law and Christian Freedom*

Summarize the fact that heresies try to make us do things that the Bible does not. They try to impose law where the Bible allows for freedom lived in love. But this freedom does not mean that we may disobey God's revealed will as taught by "sound doctrine" (v. 10). Remind the class of Kooistra's discussion of the three appropriate uses of the law of God, mentioned by Calvin. Identify them and allow some time to discuss them. Make sure the group agrees that all three of these uses of God's law are still very appropriate for today.

■ Focus 6: *Our Only Sure Defense* (1:12-20)

Call the group's attention back to the question we left unanswered in focus 2: How do we know if a certain group is a legitimate part of the body of Christ or whether it is a sect? How can we sort out heresy from the truth? Ask the class to read verses 12-20 for themselves. Discuss this question:

Q. What, according to Paul, provides us with a measuring stick to decide if a certain teaching is true or false?

In short, the gospel of which Paul is a messenger (vv. 18-19). Although he admits he was and is no sweetheart (v. 15), Paul proclaims this gospel with the Lord's authority (vv. 12-14). Its unalterable core rests in the good news that "Christ Jesus came into the world to save sinners" (v. 15) and that those who believe in him will receive eternal life (v. 16). Any teaching that detracts from that message is false. Timothy, and we, must remain faithful to that same old message in every modern age (v. 19)—the message we find in the Bible, the Old(er) and New(er) Testaments. Everything we believe and do must meet that, and only that, criterion.

■ Focus 7: *Closing*

Conclude the session with prayer. If your group feels comfortable, ask for sentence prayers seeking God's protection from false teaching for themselves, their children, your church community, and especially for those who are trapped in a sect or cult.

Options

Option 1: Face to Face

Invite a Jehovah's Witness or Mormon to your class to share the major teachings of his/her faith. Be sure to show real courtesy, since you must represent Christ to these people. Allot enough time and flexibility to your guest(s) to make his or her presentation and then allow for questions from the group. This is no time to try to convert this person or to argue him or her into a corner. Your goal will be simply to gain knowledge of another belief system and to ask biblical questions within their framework. Pray that your sensitive, honest, Bible-based questions may lead your visitor to reevaluate his or her own beliefs.

Option 2: Brass Tacks

You may wish to spend some time discussing a specific issue relating to "The List of Lawbreakers" that Kooistra mentions:

Q. Many churches distinguish between homosexual orientation and homosexual practice. Do you find this to be a helpful distinction?

The Christian Reformed Church, for one, does. It urges its churches to show full acceptance of those who, through no fault of their own, are sexually attracted to members of their own sex. However, it also teaches that Scripture clearly forbids homosexual acts (1 Tim. 1:10). It does not condemn people for their orientation. But it does help them maintain biblical standards of conduct.

Q. Is slavery still an issue today? Does it involve us?

Slavery is still practiced in many parts of the world. We need to expose it and confront it. We also need to realize that our demand for inexpensive consumer goods often causes producers to employ sweatshop workers who live in virtual bondage. As buyers we can do much to insist that employers treat their workers fairly.

We may also be guilty ourselves of treating employees or fellow workers unfairly. We need to remind ourselves that we may own the means of production but we do not own our workers. They are God's servants.

SESSION FOUR

Worship

Introductory and Background Comments for the Leader

1 Timothy 2:1-7

In 1 Timothy 1 Paul warns us to remain vigilant against false teachers who pervert the truth of the gospel. These false teachers try to place obligations on us that the Bible does not and so rob us of our freedom to serve our Lord. Paul reminds us to stay in constant touch with the gospel truth so that we may steer clear of them.

Paul also shows us that our freedom in Christ does not take away our responsibility to live our lives in his service. There are bad rules, and there are good rules. The former are those needlessly imposed on us by false teachers. The good ones are those that are clearly laid down for us by the Good News itself. One such requirement is that believers join together in worship. In 1 Timothy 2 Paul spells out some of the ways in which the Ephesian church can structure its worship to fulfill God's will. We will focus on these instructions in this session and the next.

A key element of our worship is prayer. Paul begins with that subject (2:1-7), which forms the focus of our discussion today. It is important that we realize that Paul does not try to be comprehensive in his treatment of this or any other topic. Remember, this is a letter. Paul only highlights those aspects that he considers crucial at the moment. No doubt what Paul writes here about prayer is only a small part of a much larger conversation he and Timothy shared on the subject. You may wish to supplement your group's discussion on prayer by providing a wider overview of it. But it may be wiser to spend your time in class dealing with the complex, yet fascinating issues that Paul raises.

Purpose of the Study

In his explanation of this passage Kooistra helps us to examine the *content* of our prayer. What should we say to God when we get together in public worship? What's appropriate, and what is not? What should we be sure to include?

While Paul does not intend his list to be exhaustive, this passage gives a good place to begin when evaluating our own congregational prayers. If we heed his words, we will discover a new freshness and openness as we bring the whole world and everyone in it before God's throne. Our worship does not allow us to cower behind solid oak doors as we try to hide from the world and keep God all to ourselves. On the contrary, we approach our God with all the needs of the everyday world firmly on our minds. We confess that every remote inch of it, every person in it, belongs to God. We also remind ourselves of how bighearted our God truly is: "[He] wants all men to be saved and to come to a knowledge of the truth" (2:4).

Too easily we restrict our prayers to our own narrow requirements and wants. We forget that God has not gathered us just for ourselves but includes us in his mission of reconciling the world to himself. That reality needs to be up-front and personal in our worship. Our heartfelt prayer for the needs of the world outside our church walls will keep it there. As we reflect on Paul's advice to Timothy, we will evaluate our own prayers to see if they actually honor Paul's urging.

■ Focus 1: *ACTS*

Begin this session by explaining that we will look at the content of the prayers we offer at our worship services. We will examine them in the light of the directives that Paul gives Timothy, with an eye to improving our communal conversation with God.

Ask a volunteer to read 1 Timothy 2:1-7. On the board write the word "ACTS" vertically in capital letters to form the beginning of a small acrostic. This acrostic reminds us of key elements that should show up in our prayers on a regular basis. Your participants may already know that these letters stand for ADORATION (praising God), CONFESSION (telling God we did wrong), THANKSGIVING (thanking God for his benefits to us), and SUPPLICATION (asking God to supply our needs).

Write them on the board and be sure to include these four elements in your opening prayer. Conclude the prayer by asking God to grant his Holy Spirit to us as we worship so that we may rightly bring glory to his name and be built up together as the body of Christ.

■ Focus 2: *Elements of Prayer* (2:1)

Obtain an audio- or videotape of a televised worship service. Ask the class to reread 1 Timothy 2:1 for themselves and the brief section in *Straight Talk* titled, "The Urgent Need for Prayer." Inform the participants of the theme of the service and play back all the prayers that were offered in it. (Use the tape counter or some other way of cuing the tape to the right places.) As a group analyze the contents of the prayers offered. Do they meet Paul's concerns? Do they include all four elements with which we began this session: adoration, confession, thanksgiving, and supplication? Do they *need* to do so in every service?

Allow for some reactions and discussion of the questions you raised. Be sure to point out the strengths of the prayers as well as where they might fall short. Suggest that not every service requires all the elements all the time. Paul urges; he does not give an absolute command. Ask the group what they should do if the prayers in their own worship services consistently fail to include these elements.

An appropriate response would be for them to raise the concern with the pastor or a representative of the worship committee. Recommend that they not wait until the next congregational meeting and publicly blast away at the prayer leader(s). Remind them that Matthew 18:15-20 still applies.

■ Focus 3: *Prayer for Everyone*

Remind the class that Paul urges the Ephesians to make "requests, prayers, intercession and thanksgiving . . . for *everyone*" (v. 1). Kooistra points out how difficult that becomes when we include people who have deeply hurt us. Invite class members to take a pencil and paper (have some extras around for those who are not equipped) and write down a time when they personally tried to pray for an "enemy." What happened? What did they pray for the person(s) who hurt them? Were their prayers more like the psalms that Kooistra tags "Psalms of Curse"? Or were they more in line with Paul's urging in verse 1? Ask for a volunteer or two to share their stories with the class. If no one is willing, perhaps you could share an example from your own life.

To conclude this part of your discussion, ask someone to read Luke 23:26-34.

■ Focus 4: *Prayer for All in Authority* (2:2)

Observe that Paul indeed asks us to pray for all people. However, he singles out those whom God has placed in authority over us (v. 2). Share with the class the following example of such a prayer that comes from the play *Fiddler on the Roof.*

The setting for the play is a small town in Russia before the Communist revolution. The Jewish community frequently finds itself at odds with the other townsfolk, particularly with the authorities, who conform to the anti-Jewish posture of the Russian government, all the way up the ladder to the Tsar himself. The Jews continue to scratch out a meager, precarious existence in the face of countless indignities and persecution. At one point the rabbi is confronted by a member of his community who asks him point-blank if he has a blessing for the Tsar. A dangerous question! If he does not provide a blessing, he could be in deep trouble with the already hostile authorities and condemned as a traitor to his country. If he does provide such a blessing, then he will be considered a collaborator by his own community. What should he do? His ingenious response: "Of course . . . God bless and keep the Tsar . . . *far away from us*!"

Allow some discussion on the following questions:

Q. Do you think such a prayer is in the spirit of Paul's urging in verse 2?

To the extent that it seeks God's blessing on even hostile authorities, as well as to the extent that it seeks relief from the oppression exerted by this ruler, it is. However, it falls short because it does not ask God to bring the ruling authority back to a rule that brings about justice and harmony for all, including the Jews. Verse 2 of 1 Timothy 2 recognizes that God has a purpose for giving leadership to the authorities. If they are not fulfilling that purpose as they should, then we may certainly pray for God to correct them.

Q. What is the appropriate relationship between the church and the secular government? What should we do beyond simply praying for those in authority over us?

As individual members of his body, God calls us to use our gifts and fulfill our calling everywhere. That means that we should encourage and support those who bring their Christian commitment to bear in the political arena.

As a community of believers our task is more limited. Because we are a visible segment of a higher kingdom, the kingdom of God, we should not be allied too closely with the secular authorities. However, we do have the obligation to bring the gospel into every facet of life, even into the governmental area.

As a church we should prophesy to the nations, allowing the light of Scripture to illuminate public policy. Those of us in democratic countries particularly have the opportunity and the calling to contribute our witness in that area of public life. How we can precisely work that out presents an important, if largely unanswered, challenge.

Q. Who else do we include in our prayer when we pray for "all those in authority"?

Presidents, governors, mayors, parents, teachers, church leaders, bosses, commanding officers, choir directors, among many others. God empowers each of those people to provide leadership that will benefit humankind, themselves, and the church community. It is to this community that Paul now shifts his attention.

■ Focus 5: *Prayer for the Church Community*

Point out Kooistra's observation that the end of verse 2 clearly states what should be the primary intent of our prayer for the authorities: that it may be "possible for the church to be church." By living "peaceful and quiet lives" God's people will be able to fulfill their calling "in all godliness and holiness" (v. 2); they will not be hampered by constant interference or hardship.

■ Focus 6: *Trivia Game*

Divide the class up into its warring trivia factions. Post their cumulative score on the board from previous sessions and promise that they can improve that score significantly today. Break up the groups and allow them precisely three minutes to list the names of people known to all (living or dead) who clearly exhibit both of the Christian virtues that Paul mentions: godliness and holiness.

They will score points only for those names that the other team does *not* have, so they should keep the other team from hearing their answers. Furthermore, they will only receive a point for those people whose last names begin with a *different* letter of the alphabet. So once they have a name that starts with a *C*, they should not take the time to write down another one beginning with a *C*. When you review their responses, no doubt they will dispute each others' answers. Assert your own authority as the one and only final arbiter. You're the ref; you get to score the results. Only written appeals will be received. These may be deposited directly and conveniently in the circular file.

■ Focus 7: *What God Wants* (2:3-7)

Reassemble the combatants (even if they refuse to be reconciled) and ask someone to read 1 Timothy 2:3-7. This text raises the difficult issue of whom God will save. The Bible clearly tells us that there are people who will not be saved. Kooistra cites Matthew 22:14: "For many are invited, but few are chosen." Yet Paul clearly tells us in verse 4 that God wants everyone to be saved. So if God is eternal and all-powerful, why aren't they?

Kooistra offers several possibilities but admits that the answer is not at all clear. Allow your group to kick this difficult question around for a while. You may want to conclude the discussion not by giving any definitive answer but simply by demonstrating what happens when we allow our understanding to become unbalanced. The following example may help.

We accept the biblical truth that God is sovereign and can do all things, which includes breaking through our human rebellion. That lets us put one oar in the water. We also accept the biblical truth that God has not made us robots—he has given us freedom and responsibility. That puts the other oar in the water. If we take the one seriously but not the other, then we row our boat around in circles and get nowhere. We need to affirm both—the sovereignty of God and our human responsibility—100 percent. If we don't, around and around we go.

Conclude the discussion by voicing appreciation for both sides of the issue. What's important is not that we understand how these are connected; we can leave that in God's hands. What really counts is that we hang on to both and do what we can to get the Word out to those who do not yet know it. As children of such a bighearted God we want to work and pray for the salvation of all people, even our enemies.

■ Focus 8: *Closing*

If your group has noted some areas of your worship prayers that could use improvement, delegate someone who has maturity, love, and sensitivity to raise the matter with the pastor or worship leader.

Go back to the four elements of prayer with which you started: adoration, confession, thanksgiving, and supplication. Suggest that these be included in your closing prayer. You might also suggest a guided prayer, in which you, as leader, will supply the lead-in to each part, allowing participants time to pray silently in response. You could then conclude the prayer or do so together using the Lord's Prayer.

Options

Option 1: A Proactive Effort

Ask the class to prepare a congregational prayer for next Sunday's service. Split up the group into four sections and let each one compose one of the ACTS sections. Be sure to ask your pastor for the service theme so that groups can string their prayers along that common thread. Find volunteers willing to lead the congregation in that prayer on Sunday. Be sure to ask permission from the pastor or worship leader and have him/her edit your prayer, examining all relevant details you may have overlooked.

Option 2: Consultation

Invite representatives from your worship planning team to your meeting. Tell them you are studying 1 Timothy 2:1-7 and ask them to reflect on the place of prayer in the worship service—how they structure it, what they see as its important components. You don't want a lecture from them, just some thoughts on how they deal with prayer in worship on a practical level. Allow the class some time to respond by asking questions or providing input.

SESSION FIVE

Men and Women

Introductory and Background Comments for the Leader

1 Timothy 2:8-15

After warning Timothy away from false teachers and their useless do's and don'ts, Paul begins to discuss with him what the gospel requires of those who live by God's "economy"—his house rules. In our last session we examined Paul's insistence that prayers offered in worship be as wide and inclusive in showing concern for the world as God himself is. Continuing on the theme of worship, Paul now directs his attention to the roles that women and men should play in the service (2:8-15).

The session today could get stormy. In Reformed churches we are sorely divided on our views of the role of women within the community of faith. The issue is so divisive that it has resulted in church splits and lasting bitterness between us. It will be crucial for you as a leader to allow open, honest discussion on the topic but to constantly reassert our deeper unity in Christ that must continue to bind us together despite our differences on this practical issue. Be sure to allow and respect the presentation of different views. Insist on fairness, Christian love, and a willingness to hear each other out.

You personally may not agree with the explanation Kooistra presents. Don't let that concern you. You have every right to make your own views known as long as you respect the right of others in your class to do the same. Maybe you will not find agreement in this session, and that's just fine. What matters is that you agree in the Lord, even if it means that on this issue you agree to disagree.

Your discussion will be more valuable if 1 Timothy 2:8-15 is your topic, not the women in ecclesiastical office issue. These two may be hard to separate, but here we seek to listen carefully to what the Spirit says to the churches.

Purpose of the Study

The purpose of this study is to see how a specific set of instructions for the ancient church can help us understand how to function as a church today. We will try to find out why Paul said what he said about worship roles in the context of the Ephesian church. We will also try to determine what God's abiding will is. We will look for the enduring norm that expressed itself in that specific historical form. We can then try to find an appropriate way of expressing that norm in a present-day form that obediently lives God's good news in our culture and time.

Our objective is not to gain consensus on the specific role women (or men) should play in church today. We need not agree on that point. What we do hope to accomplish, whether we agree with Kooistra or not, is to find out what Paul's central concern here can tell us about what really matters in our worship. On that issue we should be able to agree. If in the bargain we get a bit further along in our discussion on gender roles in the church, then that's a plus. But it's enough just to get your class to take seriously the cultural setting in which the Word of God was first spoken and to take that into account in our reading of what God has to say to us today.

■ Focus 1: *One in Christ*

Introduce today's topic by stating that we will be discussing the appropriate roles for women and men in worship. Emphasize that though this may be a contentious and painful issue, it may not separate us from one another or destroy our unity in Christ. Whatever our views, we will need to keep praying for the Lord to show us the way to obediently find and follow his will. That is genuinely what we all want, whatever our position happens to be.

Lead in prayer, asking God to restore unity and harmony in our churches and to help us find his will in this matter. Pray also that this session may contribute to the unity you experience as members of Christ's body.

Invite a volunteer to read 2 Timothy 2:8-15.

■ Focus 2: *Lifting Holy Hands* (2:8)

Use the following questions to help the group reflect on 2:8:

Q. Contrast the posture your group assumed as you prayed with the way Paul tells the Ephesian men to pray. What does each posture convey, and which is more appropriate?

We tend to fold our hands, close our eyes, and bow our heads. The first two gestures show our desire to focus earnestly on our conversation with God by keeping ourselves from doing or seeing something that may distract us. We bow our heads to show our humble dependence on God. The Ephesian believers raised their hands and eyes toward heaven to focus earnestly on their conversation with God by keeping themselves from doing or seeing something that would distract them. They raised their faces to heaven to show their humble dependence on God. The way they prayed and the way we tend to pray are both entirely appropriate postures at worship; six of one, half a dozen of the other.

Q. The key to Paul's directive lies in the adjective "holy"; the Ephesian men must lift *holy* hands in prayer. What does that mean?

As Kooistra explains, it means that the posture of prayer and prayer itself mean nothing unless they are consistent with the way we live. If we are at odds with each other or if we sow doubt or disputes, then our prayers will be unacceptable to God. "Holiness" in this context means that we approach our God with deep, heartfelt devotion.

Summarize for the group Paul's expectation—that men pray in all honesty and sincerity, living lives that reflect the truth of what they are saying to God.

■ Focus 3: *Role Models* (2:9-12)

Paul now turns to the participation of women in worship. He asks women to dress modestly and to show the same consistency between their lifestyle and their praying that he requires from the men (v. 10). But then Paul extends his discussion to include the role of women in the rest of the worship service. To gain a good understanding of why Paul says what he says here, we need to remind ourselves of the way in which society functioned in that time.

On the board put three headings: THEN, FIFTIES, and NOW. Ask the group to brainstorm words or phrases that describe the position of women in the Greek world of Paul's time, in the postwar era, and in our society today.

Possible descriptions for THEN would include: homebound, uneducated, property of father or husband, subservient, dependent, not highly respected, restricted to household duties, branded as prostitutes if they did not fit the mold.

For the FIFTIES we could include: homemaker, moderate level of education, considered a person, dependent on husband, greater respect, emerging freedom to take other roles, low-paid and low-level employment opportunities.

For the NOW column we might write: well-educated, mobile, greater employment opportunities, higher pay and job level, provides second income, flexible roles, higher incidence of singleness, increasingly respected as persons.

Q. Do these cultural differences change the ways in which women can participate in our church community? Should they change them?

Allow some discussion on this point, and then see if you can get some consensus on the following points:

Clearly cultural differences do change the ways in which women *can* participate in the church community. Their increased level of education, mobility, autonomy, and giftedness make them much more capable than their Ephesian sisters. Also, the radical emancipation of women that has taken place in our society has reversed the way in which society looks at participation of women in the authority structures of the church. In Paul's day such participation would have been judged scandalous. Today the reverse would be true for churches or any other institution that does not allow women to participate in leadership roles.

The second part of the question is harder to answer. Some group members may argue that these changes are worldly changes, which should not affect the way we structure the church. They believe the Bible, including 2:11-12, gives abiding directives that exclude women from such roles permanently.

Others may argue that the reasons why Paul places these restrictions no longer apply: women are now capable of teaching as well as learning; they can provide able leadership, and their doing so no longer scandalizes the world around us. They might also argue that continuing the practice of excluding women from leadership roles would raise an unnecessary barrier against modern-day nonbelievers—the very thing Paul was trying to prevent. For these reasons they would agree that change in these areas is required and biblical.

Having allowed for both of these positions, you may want to call attention to the fact that the role of women within the church community has certainly been enhanced and opened up to a great extent, allowing them to use their gifts more than ever before. All of us can agree that is a positive development. We can agree to disagree on the issue of the extent to which that process should be continued to include church offices.

■ Focus 4: *Trivia Along Gender Lines*

We hope your discussion up to this point has kept your unity intact. Now's the time to throw that to the winds, fracture your class back into its competing trivia teams. The trivia questions for this week all deal with gender roles in Scripture.

Q. Paul instructs Timothy to tell women to dress modestly in church. What hairdo does he forbid in 1 Timothy 2:9 (no peeking!)?

Braids.

Q. In verse 10 Paul tells Timothy what women at worship *should* wear. What is it (don't peek!)?

Good deeds.

Q. According to Paul, who should wear hats in church—men, women, or both?

Only women (1 Cor. 11:4-10).

Q. Does Paul think it is wrong for men to have long hair?

Yes (1 Cor. 11:14).

Q. Family trees in the Bible generally report only the names of men. One notable exception is the most important family tree of all, that of Jesus Christ, as recorded in Matthew 1. Name at least three of the four women mentioned there (no half points allotted for less!).

Rahab, Ruth, Bathsheba, Mary.

Q. Simeon and Anna both testified publicly to the identity of Jesus at the time of his circumcision (Luke 2:21-38). Of which tribe was Anna?

Asher (God allowed the ten lost tribes to witness and bear witness to the Messiah through its last faith-filled, female, senior citizen remnant).

Count up the scores and add them to the cumulative totals in preparation for next session's blistering counterattack.

■ Focus 5: *A Woman's Place* (2:13-15)

Split the class into groups of two or three. Ask each group to appoint a reporter who will record the majority opinion within the group of what Paul means to say in verses 13-15. Ask the groups to be as concise as possible in their explanations. Have them refer to Kooistra's explanation wherever they find that helpful. Reconvene the groups and ask the recorders to report in turn. Allow some freewheeling discussion without trying to nail down a definitive answer to this difficult text. Reserve enough time for focus 6.

■ Focus 6: *Prayer for Unity*

Ask your group to share briefly some of the hurts caused by our disagreement on the appropriate role of women within the church. Conclude your session with prayer, confessing our pain and where we have needlessly increased it. Ask that God will lead us to the right answer. Pray that in the meantime we may continue to work together as women and men, in love, harmony, peace, and partnership.

Options

Option 1: Panel Presentation

Assemble a panel of three or four persons to reflect on the issue of the appropriate role of women in the church. Ask panel members to give a five-minute presentation of their views and then tell them you will allow questions from the class. You may want to have the following persons represented on the panel: a church school teacher, an evangelism committee representative, an elder, an unchurched person, a female professional, a worship leader, a teenager, someone with theological training.

Option 2: Job Sharing

As a group, list all the different tasks that are routinely carried out in your church fellowship. Attach the names of those who are involved in those tasks. How does this list stack up from a gender perspective? Do men and women share the work in your church? Who carries the lion's share? Any suggestions for improvement?

SESSION SIX

Elders and Deacons

Introductory and Background Comments for the Leader

1 Timothy 3:1-13

We discovered in our last two sessions how Paul wishes Timothy to regulate worship in the Ephesian church. Paul has dealt with the content of congregational prayer and the appropriate roles of women and men in the service. He now switches to a different topic—leadership in the church. In particular, he lists the requirements for those who wish to serve as elders and deacons within the congregation. Kooistra points out the importance of this matter because these leaders must enable the church to stay true to, and live out of, the gospel truth.

Although this topic will probably not bring class discussion to a boil the way the previous one may have, the concerns of church leadership are at least as important. Kooistra observes that the time is long gone when people were eager to serve as elders or deacons. Even the sense of duty that once motivated prospective officebearers to grudgingly accept the task has broken down so that many churches face a real crisis of leadership. What should we do if we cannot find people willing and able to serve—settle for fewer leaders or drop our standards? We will have to come back to this topic in our discussion.

But first we will review Paul's criteria for judging whether people qualify for these offices. As on previous issues we will need to ask ourselves if and how these standards still apply in our churches today.

When we ask that question, we should realize that the specific task assigned to church leaders varies with time and place. Already in the New Testament we see a variety of offices that remain flexible with respect to their specific job descriptions. As Kooistra points out, the offices in the church are all basically one. All officebearers are servants, deacons in the original sense of that word. How a church specifically delineates the various leadership roles remains flexible, depending on the tasks that need doing. Even today, deacons in one church may do what elders do in another. Some churches may not even have elders or deacons. New terms are continually springing up to define new leadership roles that become necessary.

Offices such as administrator, youth pastor, and board member, to name just a few, are replacing more traditional ones such as overseer, bishop, and the like. What matters is that your church has the kind of leadership structure and the leaders that best suit its needs, optimizing its ability to fulfill its mission. This session will help your class evaluate the leadership structure in your church. If any good suggestions for improvement emerge, be sure to pass those on to your church council in a loving, helpful manner.

Purpose of the Study

In this session we want to focus on the kind of people that the Holy Spirit qualifies to serve as our leaders. What should they be like? How should we decide whom to call and to what areas of leadership?

In addition to those concrete questions we want to examine the matter of church leadership itself. What role should officebearers play in our churches? Are they the bosses, or is our church a democracy? Do we overestimate their role or underestimate it? What value should we place on church leadership? To what extent should we allow our leaders to lead?

Finally, we want to gain biblical insight into how leaders should relate to other leaders. What is the task of the elder as opposed to that of the deacon? How do we decide what kind of leadership structure we should have?

As we work through these issues, we should gain a sense of the kind of people we will want to nominate and elect for church leadership. We should also grow in our ability to discern what the roles of our leaders should be. In that way we can contribute meaningfully to the ongoing responsibility we share—to ensure that our leaders follow Christ as they show us his way.

■ Focus 1: *Leading Off*

Begin this session by introducing today's topic. Ask someone to read 1 Timothy 3:1-13. Lead the group in prayer, asking God to enrich your class with his presence and guidance. Pray especially that the leaders in your church may stick close to their Lord as they serve your fellowship.

■ Focus 2: *How Noble?* (3:1)

Remind the class of what Kooistra points out—in many churches today the status of its leadership roles has significantly declined. Church leaders are no longer respected as they once were. As a result the work of officebearers has become more difficult, and fewer candidates are willing to accept the responsibility. Ask if this is true for your church as well. If so, what could and should you do to raise the esteem and the self-esteem of your church leaders? How can your congregation support them better? Entertain some open discussion on this topic.

If your class feels there is a real lack in this area, try an "altar call." Ask them what they specifically propose to do to give encouragement and ask them to commit to actually doing it. Suggestions can extend anywhere from scheduling a leadership appreciation event (a roast?) to simply telling their elders, eyeball-to-eyeball, they appreciate their work.

■ Focus 3: *Job Descriptions* (3:2-12)

Share with the class Kooistra's observation that the Bible does not give us a specific job description for officebearers. Explain that your church *does* have such a description gleaned from the Bible and from the wisdom and experience of churches within your denominational covenant. You can find them in your church's ordination forms as well as in its church order.

Split the class up into three sections. Assign group 1 to look at the ordination form for elders; group 2, the form for deacons; and group 3, the form for ministers of the Word. (If your church divides its offices up differently, assign these tasks accordingly.) Be sure to have enough copies of the appropriate form available for each participant. (You may need to photocopy them; if you cannot find them in the back of your church's songbook, your pastor will be able to help you round them up.)

Ask each group to list on newsprint, in bullet form, the tasks entrusted to the office they are assigned. Then ask them to make a similar list of the qualifications a candidate should have. Allow them to refer to today's passage and Kooistra's book, if they wish, and, if possible, to the denominational church order. However, they should be able to think of some additional "should-haves" not mentioned in these sources.

When the groups have completed the assignment, reconvene and ask each group to post its list on the wall. Have the class review them. Allow some questions and discussion if disagreement crops up. Because the role of officebearers is "squishy," depending on when and where those in church office serve, you need not gain consensus. What is more important is that your lists are well developed enough to make sense of the following step.

■ Focus 4: *So Now What?*

Ask the group to discuss the following question:

Q. Kooistra observes that very few people, if any at all, can fulfill these requirements for office. In today's demanding world it is also true that many people who would be qualified are already over-extended and do not have the opportunity to serve. So what should we do—have fewer leaders or drop the standards of office you've listed?

This is a difficult question and an important one because councils face it every year. Very few churches manage to avoid the potential leadership crunch.

Make sure the discussion raises considerations on both sides of this issue. Dropping standards may be very unwise. We entrust our officebearers with a great deal of responsibility. Not only do they provide direction for the entire congregation in decision making, but they must also provide sound, spiritual leadership to the individual members. On top of that we expect them to lead us in reaching out to those who are not yet of the household of faith. These are awesome responsibilities. Unqualified people can cause a great deal of damage and pain to the entire community of faith as well as to individual members. A "hiccup" in the discharge of these offices may well deter nonbelievers from finding Christ.

On the other hand, maintaining high standards may mean that we cannot find enough good leaders. That situation would put tremendous stress on those who are fit to serve. They simply will not be able to do everything they are called to do. This is a formula for burnout, and consequently, the church will lose the good leaders it does have.

Observe that the Bible indicates in passages like Ephesians 4 that God will supply our need for leaders. If we have this crunch, it is obviously not because our Lord has become stingy with his gifts. We know that God does provide for our needs. However, we may have to make some strategic decisions that will allow us to make better use of the leadership gifts our risen Lord has spread throughout our churches. This notion leads to the next question:

Q. How can we make better use of the leadership gifts God has given us?

Put the suggestions offered by the groups on the board. Ask for a volunteer (or assign a "volunteer") to record them and formulate a letter to council (this will probably be homework). Offer to edit the letter before it finds its way to the clerk. Ask your council for a response to your letter so that you can share the results of its consideration with the class.

Churches have found some very creative solutions to the leadership crunch. Here are a few you may want to throw into the discussion:

- Spread the responsibility around by differentiating tasks. One example: ordain administrative elders who give leadership to the wider body and visiting elders who are responsible for supervising the spiritual life of members. The same division of labor can be applied to deacons. This type of ordination has the added advantage of better matching gifts to very different task requirements.
- Hire more paid staff to take responsibility for youth ministry, small group development, or pastoral care to seniors.
- Commission gifted people to auxiliary tasks that complement the work of the officebearers. District representatives could handle much of the kind of caregiving responsibilities that leaders are expected to give but never seem to get around to.
- Where you think it is biblically obedient to do so, extend leadership roles in your church to women.
- Provide adequate training to allow people with an interest in a certain area of leadership to pursue it before being put on the spot. A mentoring program can be very effective—seasoned officebearers "buddy up" with prospective candidates, taking them along on visits and gradually allowing the trainee to take over more and more responsibility.
- Set up a database and constantly update it by asking current members, new members, and those making public profession of faith what areas of ministry they would be interested in pursuing. Many good candidates tend to be overlooked because they are simply never identified, much less asked.

■ Focus 5: *A Pecking Order?*

Share with the class Kooistra's observation that the traditional role of deacon has been seen largely as a stepping-stone to the "higher" office of elder. Kooistra argues that this was not the case in the early church, where the offices were all considered of equal value because they were essentially one. This notion is also reflected in the fact that the requirements Paul lists for elder and deacon so closely match. Kooistra seems to agree with the modern tendency to lump the offices together under the general term of "ministry."

Ask members to take a few moments to reflect on the leadership structure of your church. Throw out some questions like the following:

- Should only elders, deacons, and pastors be represented on the council, or should evangelism committee representatives, worship leaders, teachers, and program leaders also be included?
- If they are not all included, then how should all of these church leaders synchronize their efforts?
- Who should have the most "say" in the church—elders, deacons, pastors?
- Who should be accountable to whom?

Entertain some time for open-ended discussion. Allow sufficient time to conclude this session with focuses 6 and 7.

■ Focus 6: *Trivia Game*

Suggest that it is time once again to don the boxing gloves. Highlight the cumulative score and deliver suitable praises and taunts to the combatants.

Q. The New Testament word for any and all officebearers is *diakonos,* from which we derive the word *deacon.* What does it mean?

Servant; officebearers are God's servants called to serve us by providing us with the leadership we need to ably serve our Lord.

Q. Most churches in the Reformed tradition have adopted a *presbyterian* form of church government. What does that word mean?

Elder-ruled; it comes from the Greek word *presbyteros,* which means elder.

Q. In the Reformed tradition can a congregation overrule decisions of its council or consistory?

No.

Q. In churches in the Reformed tradition can a major assembly (a classis or a synod) overrule decisions of the church council?

No. The worst it can do is disfellowship such a church from the denomination.

Q. When the early church needed to fill the position left vacant by Judas's betrayal and suicide, it used a three-step process to do so. Name at least two of these steps.

They proposed two suitable candidates, prayed to the Lord, and then cast lots between them (Acts 1:23-26).

Q. In Paul's letter to Titus he tells his apprentice that he left him in Crete to complete something Paul did not get around to doing himself. What was it?

Appointing elders (Titus 1:5).

Tally up the scores, add them to the total score, and allow some bragging and excuse-making as long as they remain good-natured.

■ Focus 7: *Closing Prayer*

Close this session by inviting the group to pray for the church leaders. Suggest that it would be good to refer to them by name or at least by category. Encourage sentence prayers. Thank God for your leaders' willingness and giftedness to serve. Confess things you may have done as members that made their task difficult. Ask God to motivate, equip, guide, and bless them as they fulfill their calling. Pray that they may enjoy their work and that it will make them grow in their faith and their walk with God.

As leader you may want to conclude the prayer yourself, allowing some time for members to pray silently about where the Lord would have them serve. You could close the prayer together, saying the Lord's Prayer or singing a suitable song.

Alternatively, you could start your prayer time by recommending that you together pray for your church leaders. Take suggestions as to what to include in the prayer. Ask someone to lead in the closing prayer or do so yourself.

Options

Option 1: Going to the Source

Invite an elder, a deacon, and possibly the pastor to come into your group and explain what they do. Allow the group to ask them some questions. Conclude by asking these leaders what you can do to help them do their task.

Option 2: Attending a Meeting

As a group attend a session of your church council. Make sure the executive knows you're coming and be prepared to be excused for those parts of the meeting that refer to confidential matters. Be sure to ascertain beforehand where to sit, whether your group is allowed to speak, and which part of the meeting would be most beneficial to attend if you do not plan to stay for the whole session. Ask group members to take notes on the various leadership roles and issues that they encounter during the meeting. Share these observations at your own class session and evaluate what you saw.

SESSION SEVEN

Paul's Poetic Postscript

Introductory and Background Comments for the Leader

1 Timothy 3:14-16

Our last few sessions have dealt with specific instructions that Paul urged Timothy to convey to the Ephesian church. As Kooistra points out, in today's brief but deeply moving passage Paul takes a breather. Before pushing on with his instructions about church order, he pauses to tell Timothy why these are important: "So that . . . you will know how people ought to conduct themselves in God's household" (3:14-15). If the Ephesians will only remember how important they are as Christ's church and how wondrous the truth they share, then they will be motivated to take Paul's urgings very seriously indeed. Because of who they are in God's family, what they do really matters.

Today's session may offer your class some welcome relief from more practical matters. We'll stand back a bit, regaining a wider perspective on what this business of being a church is all about. And we can take some time to celebrate the riches and glory of the one who has come to live in our midst.

The tone you will want to set for this session is one of celebration, worship, and unity. Concrete concerns may raise disagreements among us. But when we step back and rejoice together in what we all hold truly dear, then we can find each other in the Lord. Paul's reflective pause allows us to experience again how much more deeply our faith unites us than practical matters divide us.

In this session try to keep the group unified. Don't try to tease out differing opinions or encourage extended debates. If participants raise conflicting views, suggest that these are valid issues to which we may need to return. In the meantime we do not want to linger too long in this session on differing viewpoints. The material we can explore together here is just too rich.

Purpose of the Study

Your objective in this session is to bring unity, whereas before you have encouraged diversity. In the last few sessions your class has had opportunity to reflect on and argue some very volatile issues: gender roles in church, the place and tasks of the leadership. Now you need to bring the group back together, to show that the diversity we reveal on concrete issues need not disrupt our fellowship or cause divisions and rifts. We share such a deep, underlying unity in our precious faith that we can continue to confess together and work together. We can be one body, united in Christ. The goal of this session is not only to say that but also to experience it in the way you relate together in class.

The unity we want to experience is based on two confessions that Paul raises in this passage; it's important that your members understand them. Your objective will be to have the class review them, think about them, and assent to them. The first is Paul's identification of what the church truly is. The second is a beautifully simple, yet deeply profound, summary of the message that the church celebrates and confesses.

In short, the real purpose of this session is to experience your unity in Jesus Christ. May the Spirit of God grant you that precious gift.

■ Focus 1: *Gathered Together*

Welcome everyone to the class and allow the informal banter preceding your session to continue for some time if it is congenial and unifying. When you feel it's time to begin, give a brief introduction, explaining the difference between the main purpose of this session and the preceding ones (refer to the Background and Purpose sections above). Invite group members to help you concentrate on the rich realities Paul raises that provide the glue that allows us to stick together.

Ask someone to read today's passage from 1 Timothy and then open in prayer. Ask God to grant his Spirit so that you together may truly experience the unity of faith and love that keeps us one.

Focus 2: *What the Church Is* (3:15)

Remind the class of how Paul emphasizes the importance of what the church *does* because of what it *is*. In verse 15 he uses three key phrases to describe the church. Ask the class what they are and then post them on the board: "God's household," "the church of the living God," and "the pillar and foundation of the truth." Entertain some reflections on these terms by asking the following related questions:

Q. If the church is "God's household," does that mean it should care for its own members, for those still outside of the household of faith, or both?

Kooistra raises this issue in the context of the current debate as to whether churches should be maintenance or mission churches. This question arises because some mission-minded churches blame established churches for being complacent and too concerned with their own internal well-being. They charge that traditional churches have not intentionally sought to fulfill the great commission often enough.

We cannot deny that their criticism may be justified to a significant degree. However, Kooistra warns that we may not let the pendulum swing to the opposite extreme—seeking the lost to such an extent that we neglect those who already are in the body of Christ. Paul's image of the church as a household makes that clear. A family needs to care for those outside of itself; it has a purpose beyond its own boundary. But unless it nurtures and cares for itself, it will be of no use to anyone. It must provide for its own internal needs as well. So the church needs to care for both those within the household and those outside of it. As it invites others, it must build a strong, vibrant community into which it can enfold them.

Q. Why does Paul identify the church as belonging to "the *living* God"? Isn't that obvious?

Kooistra points out how this term is used throughout Scripture to clearly distinguish the church from all other faith communities. The church alone is the gathering of followers of the *living* God. All others find their unity in dumb, dead idols. In today's relativistic climate that's quite a claim to make, certainly not a superfluous one.

This claim provokes the accusation that we do not show enough respect for the beliefs of others. But Paul makes no bones about it. There is only one living God; either we have him or some other faith community does, but not both at the same time. While we fully respect the right of others to hold beliefs that are different than ours, we claim to be the church of the only one, true, living God, who has revealed himself so wondrously in Jesus of Nazareth. Respecting the beliefs of others does not mean that we buy them.

Q. If the church is "the pillar and foundation of the truth," why doesn't this make it infallible?

Because it is made up of fallible people. The church has failed many times to confess, bear witness to, or teach the truth. We affirm that the Bible, not the church, is the unfailing standard of truth for both our doctrine and life. When the church obediently affirms and lives out what the Scriptures teach, then it lives up to what God intends it to be. When it falters, then it's a pillar and foundation that comes dangerously close to allowing the roof to cave in. Without the renewing, cleansing power of God's Spirit, the presence of her Lord, and the firm direction of his Word, the church would long ago have collapsed into ruin. It would be unable to recover from its own fatal blunders.

■ Focus 3: *The Mystery Is Great* (3:16)

Divide the class into six groups (if you have less than six participants, split them into three groups and double their assignment). Supply every person in each group with your church's hymnal (and if you choose, supplementary songs you use routinely in worship). Assign a group to look at each line of Paul's confession in verse 16 and to pick a song that best celebrates that truth. Encourage the groups to reread Kooistra's explanation of these lines in the concluding section of chapter 7 before making their choices.

Reconvene the class and ask each group to report on the song it chose, explaining why it chose that particular song. If your class can make a joyful noise of greater fidelity than a rusty door hinge, sing these songs together. If you're not adept at music direction, ask someone beforehand to provide some leadership and/or accompaniment. Otherwise, ask the groups to read the stanzas or phrases that really stood out for them.

■ Focus 4: *Trivia Game*

Time to take a break from all this unity stuff. There's an ongoing battle to be waged—good-natured, to be sure! Split the group, post the cumulative point score, and let them strut their stuff. Today's trivia questions hover around Paul's beautiful confession, which we have just been studying in verse 16.

Q. Jesus "appeared in a body." Where is the first prediction of this event in our Bibles?

Genesis 3:15, where God curses the serpent: "And I will put enmity between you and the woman, and between your offspring and hers; he will crush your head, and you will strike his heel."

Q. Jesus "was vindicated by the Spirit." Kooistra observes that Jesus' coming in the flesh began his humiliation. What state does his vindication begin?

His exaltation.

Q. Jesus "was seen by angels." At the resurrection how many angels attended the grave when the women arrived?

Accept either one or two as an answer. Matthew records one, as does Mark. Luke mentions two. John doesn't write of any, but that doesn't mean he denies they were there.

Q. Jesus "was preached among the nations." This began to happen when the Holy Spirit was poured out at Pentecost. Name just five of the fifteen groups recorded in Acts 2 who heard the apostles speak in their own languages.

Parthians, Medes, Elamites, Mesopotamians, Judeans, Cappadocians, Pontians, Asians, Phrygians, Pamphylians, Egyptians, Libyans, Romans, Cretans, and Arabians.

Q. Jesus "was believed on in the world." The gospel of John records that when doubting Thomas stood eyeball-to-eyeball with the risen Christ, he said something to Jesus that forms the heart of our confession. What was it?

"My Lord and my God!" (Score a full point for getting either of these two phrases right—after all, if we cannot have grace in church, where can we have it?)

Q. Jesus "was taken up in glory." In Philippians 2:6-11 Paul gives another beautiful confession of his faith in his Savior. He states in verse 9 that "God exalted [Christ Jesus] to the highest place." God, according to Paul's confession, then gives Jesus something. What is it?

"The name that is above every name" (v. 9).

Tally totals. Tame braggers and whiners. Reinstitute some semblance of order and harmony.

■ Focus 5: *One in the Lord*

Guide the group's thinking back to the importance of the unity we have in Christ and of showing that unity to the world around us. Ask the class to individually read John 17:20-26 and quietly reflect on it for a few moments. When appropriate, ask the class to suggest concrete ways in which we can work for what Jesus prayed there. What should we be willing to give up for unity? What may we never give up? What can we contribute towards the visible unity of all God's people?

■ Focus 6: *Closing Devotions*

If you feel so inclined, ask the group to suggest a closing song. In prayer ask God to bring about the unity of the church that the world *must* come to see. Confess things we have done that cause needless division and that have made the world see brokenness instead of harmony. Give thanks for the measure of unity that does exist and that binds us together with believers of so many different colors and stripes. Pray that God will grant us the riches of oneness in that kind of diversity. Ask for a blessing on the concrete steps we take to live out that oneness in Christ.

Options

Option 1: A Panel of Pastors

Invite three or more pastors (or priests) from neighboring churches to speak for five minutes each on what they consider unique about the teachings and practices of their denominations. Ask them also to share what unites them with all believers. Allow time after their presentations for questions and responses.

Option 2: One Fast Chance

Hand every person in the group a single three-by-five card. Ask them to write their own confessions in the light of 1 Timothy 3:16. Challenge them not just to repeat what Paul says there. Instead, ask them to imagine that they have only this card on which they can communicate their deepest conviction to someone who has never heard of the Christian faith. They will never see that person again, so they cannot follow up or explain. Invite participants to volunteer their attempts but do not pressure anyone to do so. If you have time, ask the group to suggest which elements would be crucial to include. List these on the board. Which of these does Paul include in his confession?

SESSION EIGHT

Storm Clouds on the Horizon

Introductory and Background Comments for the Leader

1 Timothy 4:1-5

In his brief interlude Paul allowed us to catch our breath and regain our perspective. He backed away from practical church issues and let us remind ourselves of what the church really is—the pillar and foundation of truth.

The truth the church possesses and proclaims is very specific truth; it's the truth about Jesus Christ—who he is and what he is doing. This fact makes the day-to-day operation of the church so incredibly important. The way the church lives directly affects the way it embodies that truth and communicates it to a world still living in darkness.

At this point Paul returns to his practical instructions. He once again begins by giving specific warnings against heretics who try to pervert the church and the truth it represents. Paul makes it clear that false teachers often appear to be the very opposite of what they are. They seem so pious, so righteous, so dedicated. That's precisely what makes them so incredibly dangerous: they spin out demon talk (v. 1) while parading around in angels' robes resplendent with glittering halos.

We have already explored what our response should be towards heresy in general (session 3). We can summarize it quickly: Paul's means of combatting false doctrine is to stick to the Word of God (1:11; 4:5), accept only *its* teachings, and do what *it* says. We are not to go beyond that. With that admonition ringing in our ears, we can take some time to investigate the specifics of the heretical teaching that Paul describes and see if it still offers any kind of threat in our contemporary world.

In this lesson allow some latitude for your discussions to drift a bit on the topics of sexuality and our use of material things that God has provided. In a culture inundated with eroticism and advertising, it should not be too hard to demonstrate the relevance of this topic. And it will allow you to present a truly biblical approach that avoids the extremes of both overindulgence and needless self-denial. The key lies in our understanding of God as our heavenly Father, who wants his children to make happy use of his good gifts, enjoying them gratefully and responsibly.

Purpose of the Study

Your first objective will be to briefly reacquaint the class with the dangers of heresy and the way we as a church should guard against it. (One ancient proverb reminds us that repetition is the mother of learning.) Paul's return to this subject allows you to briefly review what we have learned about combatting heresy in 1 Timothy 1 (session 3): we need to know God's Word so well that we do what it says. This will allow us to measure every wind of doctrine with the standards the Bible alone can and may provide. Our confession that Jesus is Lord rings hollow unless we continue to live in the truth he brought us.

The main objective in this session, though, moves beyond this general reminder to a look at one feature of a specific heresy already plaguing the Ephesian church. We do not have enough evidence to pin down all the details of this false teaching (though many commentators like to take an informed guess). But its insistence on abstinence and asceticism (denying oneself material things) presents a feature that we find in many such teachings of the time.

Looking specifically at these elements helps us evaluate similar teachings in many heresies, including modern ones. It also cautions us not to veer into a false piety ourselves. False teaching does not always come from without. Very easily our own earnest desire to do what the Bible says becomes corrupted by a one-sided emphasis that does not do justice to the totality of scriptural teaching. We can become myopic and fall into the same trap as Bible-toting heretics.

What this means specifically for this session is that our main goal should be to find a truly biblical perspective on the two issues raised by Paul against the Ephesian heresy: the ongoing legitimacy of marriage and of enjoying the good stuff of creation, like food.

■ Focus 1: *Regroup*

Set the context for today by reminding the class of Paul's brief interlude and its content (see Background Comments above). Mention that in today's passage Paul returns to his specific instructions to Timothy. Ask a volunteer to read them aloud. Lead in prayer. Thank God for his holy Word, which allows us daily to steer our course. Ask God to allow us to understand it and to empower us to live in its fullness. Give God praise for the countless blessings he showers on us daily and ask that we may make good and generous use of these benefits. If you deem it appropriate to sing, sing.

■ Focus 2: *Has Inspiration Expired?* (4:1a)

Observe to the class that Kooistra begins with an intriguing question. He offers several possibilities about the way in which the Holy Spirit "clearly says" (v. 1) what will happen in later times. One way is through Scripture. Another way is by direct revelation to Paul himself. In this context Kooistra wonders aloud if it is a valid distinction to speak of the Holy Spirit *inspiring* Bible writers while merely *illuminating* those who came after them. He writes that "we need to reflect anew on how the Holy Spirit still speaks to us today."

The following questions are intended to help you do that. Discuss them with the class.

Q. What do we mean when we confess that the Bible was inspired?

We mean that the Holy Spirit carefully supervised the work of Scripture writers. He made sure that what they wrote authoritatively and accurately conveys God's revelation to us. The term "inspired" refers to what Paul writes in 2 Timothy 3:16, where he calls all Scripture "God-breathed." That this took place through the operation of the Holy Spirit we find in 2 Peter 1:21: "For prophecy never had its origin in the will of man, but men spoke from God as they were carried along by the Holy Spirit."

Q. Did the Holy Spirit also inspire Augustine to write his *Confessions*, Calvin to write his *Institutes*, and our pastor to write last week's sermon? Or did the Holy Spirit stop inspiring people after Scripture became complete?

This answer depends on what we include in the term "inspired." If we mean can and does the Holy Spirit still speak through believers today, the answer is "of course!" The Spirit never stops working. He still breathes new life into weak, sinful, old (and young) bones. He does it through the words of parents, friends, teachers, and anyone who can speak the truth in Christ, even older sisters and kid brothers! Whenever we share the words of life, we do so not in our own power but through the inspiration of the Holy Spirit.

However, when we apply the word "inspiration" to the Scriptures, then we use it in a way that includes some unique features that our inspired words do not include.

First, the Bible writers were inspired to write in such a way that they did not mess up. Their testimony is completely and totally reliable. It is "infallible," "unfailing." They never let us down. We can rely for our soul's salvation on their message. We cannot say the same thing about our inspired writings. Sometimes we score. Often we don't. Ask pastors if they have ever launched a turkey from the pulpit. If any tell you they haven't, avoid their church like a toothache.

Secondly, the inspiration of the Bible writers was unique because their testimony was based on the actual eyewitness accounts of what Jesus Christ said and did. No matter how ingenious our efforts, we can never speak with that kind of authority because we were not there when Jesus fully made God known, nor have we ever been able to talk with anyone who was.

Thirdly, since the Holy Spirit has already fully revealed all we need to know about God through the Word made flesh, our inspired writings will not add more information to what we already have. Our efforts may call and guide people back to scriptural truth. Or we may help them to see it in a new light. But we cannot add to what has already been revealed. Jesus clearly promises that his Spirit will lead us further into the truth that he has already made known. So all our inspired writings may indeed speak the words of God but only in a derivative sense. They can only speak the words of God after him. We can keep bringing good news, but it remains the good old news of Jesus and his love.

■ Focus 3: *Can We Lose Our Faith?* (4:1b)

You will want your group to discuss briefly the point Kooistra raises in connection with verse 1b, which states, "Some will abandon the faith and follow deceiving spirits and things taught by demons." These words prompt Kooistra to raise the question, "Is it possible for believers to lose their faith?" This is a difficult question and has provoked fierce, ongoing debate between many Christians. You will not need to answer it definitively, but you will want to have your group briefly evaluate Kooistra's answer to it.

At this point ask your group to switch gears. After prompting us to look at how the Spirit still speaks to us today, verse 1 puts us squarely into a very different dilemma. It states clearly that "some will abandon the faith." Does this mean that true believers can lose their faith? If so, then what is left of our assurance that we will always belong to Christ? Does this make our eternal well-being dependent on our own, ongoing, good behavior?

Ask participants to provide scriptural reasons that seem to indicate that we can indeed lose our faith. Allow them to refer to their Bibles and to Kooistra's text if they wish. Put their responses on the board in bullet form. Then ask them to provide biblical evidence that would argue the opposite. Summarize these on the board as well.

Evidence of people losing their faith can be seen in Judas's betrayal of Jesus as well as in the hundreds of warnings against falling away (Rom. 11:21; 1 Tim. 4:1b; Heb. 6:4-6). Evidence for the opposite can be found in the following passages: John 10:27-28, Psalm 125:1, and Ephesians 2:4-10.

Kooistra suggests a way to reconcile these seemingly contradictory texts. Is the class satisfied with his answer? Kooistra suggests that those who fall away came close to, but never actually received, true faith: "They stand at the gate but do not enter." That interpretation seems to reflect the understanding of the apostle John in his first letter. There John agonizes over the fact that a group of people have left the community of faith to espouse false teachings. He writes, "They went out from us, but they did not really belong to us. For if they had belonged to us, they would have remained with us; but their going showed that none of them belonged to us" (1 John 2:19). Jesus' parable of the sower also gives three examples of those who initially respond to the gospel but in whom the Word does not come to full maturity. Therefore, it never blossoms into true faith.

If Kooistra's answer satisfies the group, fine. If not, ask for other suggestions of how we can reconcile these biblical givens. It is not your objective here to arrive at a definitive answer. Allow some discussion but suggest that class members interested in pursuing this matter will need to do so as homework. You have to move along to more practical matters, such as sex and food.

■ Focus 4: *Hypocritical Lies* (v. 2-3)

Paul targets the "hypocritical liars" who teach people to abstain from marriage and from eating certain foods. To facilitate discussion, it will be very helpful to know what Paul means by the word "hypocrite."

Divide the class into three groups. Equip group 1 with a current dictionary, a Bible dictionary, and a concordance. Provide group 2 with a few commentaries on the passage we are studying (1 Tim. 4:1-5). (You can obtain these materials from your church librarian or pastor.) Ask group 3 to look at Matthew 23. Then ask the groups to list words or phrases from the materials they have been assigned that describe a hypocrite. Ask them also to explain how their descriptions might apply to the false teachings Paul describes in verses 2 and 3.

Reconvene the class and ask each group to report on its findings. Summarize the descriptions on the board and allow some questions and discussion about the way these characteristics could apply to this passage. Some of the following ideas may emerge.

Current dictionaries define the word "hypocrite" as a person who pretends to be what he or she is not. Matthew 23:3, 5 picks up on this idea; describing hypocritical people, it says, "They do not practice what they preach. . . . Everything they do is for men to see." This description also applies to the heretics against whom Paul warns Timothy, who give the appearance of being very pious and God-fearing in their self-denial.

While Christians often need to practice self-denial in order to achieve a higher purpose, they should never practice it for its own sake. If they do, they turn up their noses at the good gifts our heavenly Father wants them to enjoy. True godliness makes us celebrate our relationship with God as grateful children of a loving and generous Father, not endure it stoically as slaves trying to appease a demanding and tightfisted tyrant.

We can discover a second characteristic of a hypocrite when we look at the original meaning of the words that make up the word. *Hypocrite* comes from two Greek words—*hypo,* meaning "under" or "less than," and *critos,* meaning "judge." Putting those two together gives us something like the following meaning: "substandard judges" or "underdiscerning." Jesus expresses it so starkly in Matthew 23:24 when he says, "You blind guides! You strain out a gnat but swallow a camel."

In Timothy 4:2-3 Paul accuses the false teachers of this same vice: they lack sound judgment because they force God's people to concentrate on unimportant things, making them neglect that which is crucial. In verse 2 Paul makes this explicit, stating that their "consciences have been seared as with a hot iron"; they have frittered away their ability to discern and judge correctly.

A third characteristic of hypocrites is the needlessly heavy burden they place on others, while avoiding such burdens for themselves. As Jesus says in Matthew 23:4, "They tie up heavy loads and put them on men's shoulders, but they themselves are not willing to lift a finger to move them." In the context of Paul's warning to Timothy, such hypocrites would try to rob the Ephesian Christians of the freedom they have in Christ. They would forbid them to enjoy the salvation God gives them out of sheer grace. Avoidance of material things, as Kooistra points out, is a burden we need not carry. Such things are "consecrated by the word of God and prayer" (v. 5).

■ Focus 5: *Trivia Game*

Once the class is clear on why this false teaching is so hypocritical, divide the group along "trivial" lines. Broadcast cumulative totals and let the fur fly.

Q. What's the traditional term for the practice of remaining unmarried?

Celibacy. (Answers like "goofy" or "intelligent" score no points.)

Q. Name a Polish-pontiff-pastored portion of Christian people pursuing this practice (of celibacy).

Roman Catholic priests.

Q. The Bible, in many passages, forbids sexual intercourse outside of marriage. But does it discourage or encourage this practice *within* marriage?

It encourages it: Genesis 1:28 and 1 Corinthians 7:1-6.

Q. Is there *any* food that Paul says we should not eat?

Yes. All foods that would cause our fellow Christians to be distressed and destroyed (Rom. 14:14-15).

Q. What's the traditional term describing the sin of overindulging in food?

Gluttony. ("Pigging out" is not an acceptable answer. Your group may be interested to know that that expression is unfair to pigs. They don't overeat like humans do.)

Q. Kooistra tells us that Paul contrasts the terms "spirit" and "flesh." But he does not equate the word "flesh" with the word "body." So what does Paul mean by "flesh"?

"Our sinful nature, body and soul shackled by the power of evil" (Kooistra's words).

Tally up the results of your trivia game. Remind the class of the stakes—losers buy donuts at the last session.

■ Focus 6: *Thanks* (v. 4-5)

Once you have restored some semblance of order, ask the group what Paul's one condition is for enjoying God's good gifts. Verses 4 and 5 clearly indicate that we are to receive these gifts *with thanksgiving*. Entertain some discussion on the following questions.

Q. Does thankfulness come naturally to us or must we learn it?

Q. What obstacles prevent us from really being grateful to God for his gifts?

Q. Can you give an example from your own life or from someone else's where you have still been able to show thankfulness despite hard times?

Q. We need to constantly remind ourselves to express our gratitude to God. What's worked for you?

There are no hard-and-fast answers to these questions. Allow participants lots of free rein but try to steer the discussion away from argument. Ask some of those who speak least for their suggestions as well.

■ Focus 7: *Closing Prayer*

Conclude with a closing prayer in which you ask participants to share sentence prayers for the benefits they received from the Lord this day. Alternatively, take suggestions from the group for reasons for thanks, and ask someone to close in prayer including these items. End the prayer with praise to God as the source of all good things.

Options

Option 1: Serving Singly

Invite a Roman Catholic priest, a monk, or a nun to your class to discuss the practice of celibacy. Be sure you and your class show due sensitivity. Although you may disagree with imposed celibacy, remember that you speak with fellow believers in Christ who exclude the possibility of marriage so that they may devote themselves fully to the service of their Lord. That deserves respect, if not agreement.

Option 2: A Balancing Act

By warning us away from material things, the "hypocritical liars" in Ephesus intend to focus our attention on the "spiritual" world. Ironically, denying ourselves the good things God has given us does the opposite. Anyone who has been on a strict diet can readily testify to that. Deny yourself food, and you can concentrate on nothing else. Of course, we can also be overly involved with material things so that we are equally obsessed with them. How do we strike the right balance?

Ask group members to respond to this question by writing an advice column for their local newspaper. Ask them to keep their offering under two hundred and fifty words and to share their efforts with the class.

SESSION NINE

Timid Timothy

Introductory Comments and Background for the Leader

1 Timothy 4:6-16

Our last session allowed us to revisit the ever-present danger of heresy, which easily strikes at the very core of the precious truth that the church may celebrate and proclaim to the world. Paul urges Timothy to combat the hypocritical liars who forbid certain foods and marriage. Such practices motivate us to reject good gifts that our heavenly Father wants us to enjoy. In the process we begin to think of ourselves as more holy than others; we drift into self-righteousness by following rules we have dreamt up for ourselves. That is not the way to pursue true godliness.

Now Paul commands Timothy to train himself to be *really* godly and to exhort his fellow believers to do the same. That won't be easy for the timid evangelist. Timothy needs Paul's strong encouragement to be assertive, to take the lead and not to let others derail his ministry. Paul says that some people may find Timothy too young for his task but that his faithful practice will confirm what he preaches. Besides, Timothy has clearly shown his gifts for this task. He has received the confirmation of his calling from the "body of elders" (v. 14). As he continues to bring the word of life, training himself and his congregation in true godliness, he will save himself and those who follow his lead (v. 16). Paul urges Timothy to boldly and aggressively pursue his mission because it's a matter of eternal life and death.

In today's session we will focus on the concept of training ourselves to be godly. Training extends beyond learning. It pushes us to hone and stretch our acquired skills. Athletes train in order to stay in shape and to extend their abilities. Believers are also in training. They train for true godliness, stretching it out and extending it to every area of their lives.

We will also revisit Paul's understanding of the scope of God's salvation. Whom does he save—only believers or also nonbelievers? The provocative nature of the "trustworthy saying" to which he alludes in verses 9 and 10 provides us with some interesting discussion material. It will require you to allow more latitude in the discussion than the previous focus on training to be godly, which requires a tighter leash.

In exploring God's reach in this world, we encounter deep mysteries we cannot fully understand. But in our reflections we can tune ourselves to the very heartbeat of God. As a leader you will want to set the tone for this discussion by suggesting that the class allow you to keep it more devotional than argumentative. Discourage drawn-out debates on differing viewpoints, which may emerge. Try to find consensus on what Paul's words really mean to tell us about the broad sweep of God's salvation plan.

Kooistra concludes this chapter with a look at Paul's encouragement of timid Timothy. Too easily our own insecurity and lack of self-confidence can prevent us from fulfilling what God has specifically equipped us to do. We need a solid reality check to prod us onward to courageously follow God's call.

Purpose of the Study

As we have noted, Kooistra's discussion of this passage helps us touch on three important features of Paul's exhortation to Timothy.

The first is the importance of training in godliness. Our objective here is not to arrive at a good theoretical definition of this phrase. Rather, we want to consider ways in which we can pursue such training in godliness ourselves. The aim is to clarify what true piety is so that we can practice it concretely in our everyday lives. We want to take a hard look at our lifestyles to see if they genuinely embody godliness.

Our second goal is to reflect on the reason for living that way: the hope we have of eternal life. Living near to the heart of God inspires our godliness. When we look at the uniqueness and generosity of God's salvation, then we find the inspiration and motivation to live transformed lives.

Finally, we want to confront our tendency to sell ourselves short. Timid Timothy might all too easily shirk his responsibilities because he fears his own inadequacy. We could do the same. When we lose sight of the ways in which God renews, gifts, and empowers us to fulfill his calling, we easily underestimate what we can and should do for the coming of his kingdom. Our inferiority complexes keep us unproductive. They stunt our natural growth and development as people grounded in God's Word and invigorated by his Spirit. So we want to examine closely who we are, what God is doing in our lives, and what he will let us do in his kingdom.

■ Focus 1: *Off the Starting Block*

To open this session, ask participants to pair off and share with each other one way that they would like to grow spiritually or improve their devotional lives. Then ask partners to pray for each other, that they may meet that desire.

■ Focus 2: *In Training*

Invite someone to read 1 Corinthians 9:24-27 and discuss the following questions as a means of investigating what Paul means by urging Timothy to "train yourself to be godly" (v. 7).

Q. Does the word "training" mean the same as the word "learning"? What's the difference?

The word "training" does not mean simply to come to knowledge or understanding. It implies a sustained effort of keeping oneself in shape. Learning may or may not require action. Training always does. The passage from Corinthians alludes to the rigors that athletes undergo in keeping themselves in peak condition. Meeting this goal requires sacrifice, energy, and persistence. So does the exercise of godliness.

Q. What does Paul mean by godliness?

Kooistra distinguishes Paul's meaning of the word from that of otherworldliness and unrealistic spiritualism. He also distinguishes it from that of a lifestyle that is so earthy it loses its Christian character. Kooistra describes godliness as "living a full Christian life in the present reality," one that transforms not only our hearts but our culture as well. In describing his upbringing, Kooistra shares his own experience of godliness as modeled by his parents. From his mother he learned the depth of the soul's relationship to its Maker; from his father, the width of that relationship as it extends to every nook and cranny of our lives. Together, the Kooistras were a godly couple.

Q. Whom do you know who has demonstrated this kind of godliness?

Allow members of the group to share some anecdotes. Ask them to be specific about the characteristics that demonstrate the walk these persons enjoyed with their God.

Q. What kinds of exercises or disciplines can we follow to keep ourselves in peak spiritual condition? (You'll want to put class members' responses on the board.)

You may get a lot of good suggestions. Among them might be Scripture reading, Bible study, worship, prayer, meditation, and spiritual direction. Suggestions should also include such things as small group meetings, church education classes, participation in a specific ministry, and further training in developing spiritual gifts. If you extend the circle even further, you could also include witnessing, participating in evangelism, and involvement in Christian schools, professional groups, service projects, organizations, and agencies. Be sure group members list not only *in*tensive means of exercising their godliness but also *ex*tensive ones, because both dimensions are important aspects of true piety.

■ Focus 3: *Universalism Revisited*

Kooistra points out that verse 10 raises once again the question of whether God will actually save all people or only those who believe. Ask the class to refer to the text and summarize briefly the options Kooistra suggests for solving the problem. Ask for a straw vote to see which of these options your class members find most satisfying. Allow them to briefly explain why they voted as they did, but do not enter into an extended discussion on that issue.

More to the point is the *reason* why Paul speaks of God as "the living God, who is the Savior of all men" (v. 10). The key word we find in the beginning of that verse is "hope." Explain that Paul has been arguing that physical training will only give (modest) temporal results. In contrast, training in godliness has a very rich payoff that extends into eternity. Gold medals sufficiently motivate Olympic athletes to accept the rigors of years of training. What will motivate us to accept the discipline of godliness? Paul points to the rich reward that awaits us. Because Christ is the *only* Savior, training ourselves to live forever in his presence is simply the only game in town.

In verse 12 Paul summarizes what that spiritual training involves. He tells Timothy to model it for his congregation: "Set an example for the believers in speech, in life, in love, in faith and in purity."

Divide the class into five groups and assign each group one of these areas that require spiritual training: speech, life, love, faith, purity. Ask each group to develop a *realistic*, weekly training program that allows them to keep the spiritual aspect of their lives healthy, strong, and growing. Ask them to include the types of exercises that are necessary, the amount of resources to spend on each, and any other factors that enter into a training regimen. These might include scheduling, coaching, accountability, and measurement of progress. Reconvene the class and have each group share its results. Allow for some freewheeling discussion in which the class evaluates the efforts of each group. Conclude with this question:

Q. When all five training schedules are added together, do they still form a realistic program? How do we create room in our schedules for such spiritual exercise?

Allow some latitude in the discussion but don't let it get hung up on a single point. Try to elicit lots of suggestions and put the good ones on the board.

■ Focus 4: *Spiritual Sports Trivia*

Back to battle. Line up the opposing troops, post the cumulative score, and fire away.

Q. Some people have taken spiritual training to an extreme. Who lived for decades on top of a single pillar?

Simon Stylites.

Q. What, according to Buddhism, is the only way to full unity with God?

Meditation.

Q. Apart from their daily tasks, monks in the Middle Ages had to come together to worship and pray many times throughout the day and the night as well. How many times in a twenty-four-hour day did they assemble?

Seven.

Q. What did they call their evening services?

Vespers.

Q. True or false: What we do for a living is part of our spiritual lives.

True.

Q. Will we get to heaven without the practice of godliness?

No. Godliness is not what saves us; God is (4:10). However, godliness is a necessary consequence of his saving work in our lives (1:8-11; John 15:1-2). If we are saved, it *will* be there.

Tally the results of your game, and if a real rout is shaping up, warn the losing side to start saving their nickels for the donuts.

■ Focus 5: *Encouragement*

Remind the class how Paul had to encourage Timothy to exercise his God-given gifts.

Q. From what Paul tells Timothy in verses 11-16, what does Timothy's prime obstacle appear to be in carrying out his task?

Paul's extensive response indicates that it was not laziness or disinterest. It was Timothy's tendency to put himself down. Timothy did not sufficiently recognize his own gifts or the authority of his calling. Timid Timothy could too easily allow himself to be pushed aside by those who found him too young, too immature, or too quiet.

Q. How can your church do a better job of giving people the courage to exercise their God-given gifts?

List on the board the suggestions that the group contributes. Your church might need to pick up its socks on such things as

- identifying areas of giftedness early through an ongoing gifts-assessment program.
- affirming on a regular basis the gifts of members in visible ways.
- providing training for gift development.
- developing an apprenticeship program by buddying up rookies with experienced people who do the task well.
- confirming members in their calling by officially appointing and commissioning them.
- structuring ongoing evaluation, feedback, and accountability for every task in the church.
- broadening the kinds of ministries for which your church can and will take responsibility.
- building ministries around gifted people instead of shoehorning people into premolded slots.

If the group reaches consensus on some of its suggestions and feels strongly about them, suggest that they appoint a member to communicate this concern to council in an encouraging way.

■ Focus 6: *Closing*

Conclude the session by pointing out how our own feelings of unworthiness often make us stay mute when we have the opportunity to bring the gospel into the lives of friends, neighbors, or work associates who do not know the Lord. Paul writes Timothy that sharing the good news is a matter of spiritual life or death. So we should not stay silent.

Ask someone to read Philippians 2:12-16a. In closing prayer ask participants to thank God for the many gifts with which he has blessed your fellowship. Confess where you as a church have shut down or shut out the use of such gifts. Ask the Lord to continue supplying the gifts we need to serve well for the coming of his kingdom.

Options

Option 1: Lifestyles

Ask group members to reflect on those aspects of their lifestyles that show nonbelievers that they are godly people. Have them list in one column the don'ts of such a lifestyle. Then make a list of the things that we should do. Ask participants to share the results and spend some time discussing areas where they do not agree.

Option 2: Savior of All?

You may decide that it's time to really chew on the doctrinal issue of whom God ultimately saves and whom he does not. You may wish to deal more extensively with Paul's words in verse 10 and see how they fit into a wider biblical picture. Invite your pastor, a Bible teacher, or someone else who is theologically conversant to reflect on his/her understanding of this verse for, say, ten minutes, after which you can ask him/her to entertain questions and responses from the group.

Option 3: What About Me?

If you sense that your group is ready to do so, ask members to share their own stories of times when they felt discouraged from using their gifts. How did they respond? Have the conditions for utilizing their gifts improved?

SESSION TEN

Paul on Pastoral Care (1)

Introductory and Background Comments for the Leader

1 Timothy 5:1-16

At the last session we drew some practical applications for our lives from Paul's advice to Timothy. Paul urged Timothy to keep up his training in godliness so that he could continue his ministry of telling and showing his flock the only way of life. Training would also help Timothy to overcome his own timidity, which might cause others to shunt him aside.

In today's passage Paul continues his advice about the way Timothy should perform his task as an evangelist. Paul says that Timothy needs to treat the members of the Ephesian church not only boldly but also pastorally. Paul sensitizes Timothy to the varying approaches he should take in relating to the subgroups in his flock. Different relationships present different pitfalls, which a pastor must avoid, or the task of boldly applying God's Word will fall on deaf ears.

While he mentions five such subgroups, Paul dwells at length on the subject of widows and how the community of faith should treat them. Widows in Paul's day found themselves in dire straights. Because women were kept financially and socially dependant on their fathers, husbands, or grown sons, widows who had no such men in their lives were cut off from financial support. Even if they belonged to the lucky few who were left with sufficient funds, they would still have to bear the trauma of their loss, and they could easily be victimized. Widows remained defenseless in a society that viewed women as property. The rule of law did little to protect them because the word of women was not considered reliable in court.

As a result Paul impressed on Timothy the importance of recognizing the worth and the legitimate need of these women. In the church there can be no such downgrading of anyone who belongs to Christ—Jew or Gentile, master or slave, male or female. Furthermore, when we recognize the full value of these sisters in the Lord, we realize our responsibility to see that they receive adequate care and that, in turn, they are challenged and enabled to use their gifts in God's service within the community.

Because the circumstances of widows varied so remarkably in his day, Paul takes the time to instruct Timothy in how the community should respond in kind. That he devotes so much space to this issue demonstrates how important Paul considers this matter. For us, too, it's urgent that the church community consistently pays due attention to its weakest members. Do we?

Purpose of the Study

The purpose of this session is two-fold. On the one hand, we want to examine the ways in which Paul instructs Timothy to treat those under his care. We can learn much from the way in which Paul identifies these relationships. His instruction encourages us to examine our own relationships to see how we're doing.

On the other hand, we want to take a good deal of time trying to understand Paul's advice concerning the widows as a way of helping us become sensitive to their needs in our time. While in some countries, governments and pension plans have made life much easier and safer for widows, their loss still requires a loving, substantial response from God's people.

But Paul's instructions about the treatment of widows has a much wider scope. He singles out the socially weakest, most vulnerable members of the church. Not even slaves were in as difficult a position as these women. At least their masters would take care of them to some degree, if not because of legal obligation then at least out of self-interest. But the widow would often have no one to look out for her. By studying the response Paul urges the church to take, we can learn two things: how to identify those brothers and sisters who are in greatest need and how we can structure our faith community to meet them in that need.

■ Focus 1: *Beginning the Search*

Remind the class that Paul has laid down rules governing the task of elders and deacons. In our last session we noted how Paul turned his attention to Timothy's role as an evangelist. He encouraged Timothy to boldly bring the gospel by word and godly example. He now continues his consideration of Timothy's pastoral role in the community. In the process Paul extensively addresses how Timothy should ensure proper treatment of widows, the most needy and vulnerable of God's children in the Ephesian congregation.

Invite someone to read today's passage. In opening prayer, praise God for the wondrous way in which he works to make us one in Christ. Thank God for the many resources he has showered on us. Ask forgiveness for our inattention to the needy among us. Seek his direction as we try to identify those in our community with whom we may share. If you wish, conclude the prayer with an appropriate song such as "Jesu, Jesu" (*Psalter Hymnal* 601) or the song "Brother, Let Me Be Your Servant."

■ Focus 2: *Different Strokes*

Point out Kooistra's observation that "Paul considers the congregation to be a family, a household of faith." In 5:1-2 the apostle extends that image to four classes of people with whom Timothy will have to relate. Ask your class to take some time to draw out the implications of what this should mean for the ways we treat different groups of people in church. We need to think this through because the level of dysfunctional families is growing, and we cannot simply assume any longer that we understand what these implications are.

Invite participants to scribble down what such family relationships should mean in the way we treat each other in the Christian community. Does the analogy of a family hold up with respect to all the various relationships we encounter there, or does it break down somewhere?

Take some time to share responses. If the question does not arise in the discussion, ask what needs to change in the way we treat each other in worship, in congregational meetings, in committees, and in the various ministries of the church. This is a big question and an important one. But keep an eye on the clock; you won't be able to treat this exhaustively. A number of concrete examples will have to do.

■ Focus 3: *There's Family and Then There's Family*

Discuss with the group Paul's concern for widows by observing that the church is the family of God but that this fact does not wipe out the importance of biological and sociological families. These bonds, as well as the obligations attached to them, may and must continue in the household of faith. Children must still honor their parents. Relatives still have the primary duty to care for their kinfolk.

Ask the person who read the passage to the class to reread 5:3-8. Ask for some discussion on the following question:

Q. To what extent may we rely on the church, the state, or other agencies to care for our needy relatives?

This is a complex issue. Is it wrong to expect a laid-off brother to draw unemployment insurance? Is it all right to let a sister who is a single mom go on welfare, only topping off her income where necessary? Should we rely on the government to house our elderly parents or grandparents? Or should we meet these needs ourselves before turning to the state or the church?

Paul's rule for the church (vv. 3-4) might, at face value, be applied to the state as well. Some church communities even go so far as to forbid their members from taking out insurance of any kind. They expect victims to trust in God to supply their need and, where necessary, the church to step in.

Most believers do not follow this course. They recognize that other social entities, such as insurance companies, pension plans, and government services are legitimate means of meeting the needs of our more vulnerable members. By paying premiums and taxes, we invest in wider plans to care for those hit by crippling need. Because we participate in funding these means of provision, we also have the right to make use of them ourselves and to expect our family members to receive support from them as well.

However, we still need to hear Paul's admonition. Family bears the primary responsibility to see that adequate resources are made available to hurting relatives. And no amount of monetary income can fulfill the social and relational needs of our loved ones. They need us to be family in more than name or pocketbook.

■ Focus 4: *Family Trivia*

The trailing trivialists have only this session and next to redeem themselves. They're still expected to bring the donuts to the last session. You will show no grace or mercy in this struggle—maybe.

The questions today hover around family matters. The Bible presents us with a lot of interesting facts about them.

Q. True or false: the Bible never refers to Adam as "the son of God."

False (Luke 3:37).

Q. True or false: God punishes the children for the sins of their parents.

False. He may have had to for a while (Ex. 20:5), but he doesn't anymore (Ezek. 18:20).

Q. The Bible tells us that Mordecai raised Esther because she was an orphan. How were they related?

They were cousins (Esther 2:7, 15).

Q. At the conclusion of the book of Job we read that God gave Job another seven sons and three gorgeous daughters (42:13, 15). Job paid his daughters a courtesy that was very unusual in those days. What was it?

He "granted them an inheritance along with their brothers" (42:15).

Q. Did Jesus' brothers ever marry?

Yes (1 Cor. 9:5).

Q. According to Hebrews 12 what makes us so sure we are true children of God?

Hardship (12:7ff.).

Tally the totals. Next week's game will be the deciding bout, unless one team has fallen so far behind that recovery is impossible. If you dare to lop off some points here or there to make the final match at least a horse race, that's your call. You're on your own to invent a good excuse for doing so.

■ Focus 5: *The Served Remain Servants Too*

Introduce the next point by offering the comment that if all living cells were independent, there would be nobody around to discuss the point. Cells that are independent do not need each other and therefore do not clump together to create larger organisms. Of course, cells that only leech the elements of life from others and give nothing in return simply destroy the organism; they're called cancer cells. What makes larger organisms possible are cells that are *interdependent*.

This is a good metaphor for the body of Christ. The Holy Spirit liberally distributes the riches of our ascended Lord among God's people. But he has given no one all the gifts. That way we all need each other, and we stick together so that we can share in the common good. Our goal as members of Christ's body should not be to remain either dependent or independent but interdependent.

What this means for the sociologically and economically weaker members among us is that they really are no different than the rest of us. We all need nurture, guidance, and help from others to develop and sustain our lives. In turn, we also need to contribute to the well-being of others. So when we have given assistance to sisters or brothers in need, we have not yet done enough. We need to provide for their needs in such a way that they, in turn, can lend support to us or to others.

That is what Paul illustrates so powerfully in this passage: he instructs Timothy to put widows to work. Although they have lost their husbands, they are still created in the image of God and called to service in our Lord's kingdom. We need to equip and commission them to do so. We may not leave them stuck in their grief or imprisoned in unproductive idleness. How we do that depends on their circumstances. It means one thing for an older widow, another for a younger one. That principle also applies to all who have special needs.

Divide the class into three groups and let each one respond to the following case studies. Be sure to photocopy the studies for all participants so that they can refer to them as needed.

Case 1: Grief-Struck

Mary lost her husband, a well-to-do and retired bone surgeon, two years ago. Although she is a very capable person with no financial concerns, Mary has not come to terms with her husband's death. She lives alone and will not hear of moving or of dispensing with any of his possessions. Mary has a son, a missionary in Zimbabwe, who faithfully contacts her. He makes weekly phone calls when he can get through and writes letters, which usually take two months to arrive. Mary has no other relatives who live close enough to be of much use. She spends most of her time at home feeling lonely and at loose ends. She faithfully attends church if and when a friend picks her up. She has a car and is a confident driver but feels she has nowhere to go. What should her church do?

Case 2: Between Jobs

George is thirty-three years old; he has a wife and three children. Since high school he's been a welder but has recently lost his job and has few prospects of finding another. He collects unemployment and spends much of his time at home because he despairs of finding another job. The endless stream of rejections has drained his energy and ruined his self-esteem, and he seems headed for deep depression. He watches TV most of the day, which drives his wife around the bend. She tries to help make ends meet by doing some extra baby-sitting, but spending endless hours with toddlers, financial woes, and the couch potato, she finds the house much too crowded. There's no money for basics, let alone for Christian school tuition. What should the church do?

Case 3: Single Parent

Joan recently divorced her husband because of his alcoholism, abusiveness, and—what broke the camel's back—his marital unfaithfulness. She has full custody of their two preschoolers. Although her husband must legally pay alimony and child support, she knows she will never see one thin dime. She receives welfare but cannot afford the rent. How should the church respond?

Sharing Strategies

After they have had some time to brainstorm these case studies, call the groups back together. Ask each one to read its case study for the whole class and share suggestions about how the church should respond. Allow adequate time for feedback. Pass along to your deacons' board or your council any good suggestions the groups come up with that could help your church better meet the needs of people in difficult situations like these.

Here are some possible suggestions that may emerge for each case. If they don't, toss them into the discussion.

Mary needs some solid counseling because she is not moving through the grief process. While she can afford to pay for this herself, she needs convincing and encouragement that counseling will benefit her. She will also need a referral to a reliable agency and ongoing supportive pastoral care. Mary could benefit greatly from inclusion in a small group and a seniors' program. She will probably require a person willing to drive her and accompany her to these gatherings. Also, she needs to be invited to engage in the ministry of the church. Many churches have found widows like Mary to be tremendous resources, by officially appointing them as district visitors, by mandating them to make official welcome and hospital visits, and by asking them to represent the church at anniversary, baptism, and birthday celebrations. In the process the widows benefit greatly themselves. Their service becomes its own rich reward.

George and his family need empathetic support, not condemnation. A recognition of the devastation caused by this ordeal needs to be constantly communicated, and pastoral care maintained. Financial assistance will probably be welcome. In addition, many churches have appointed a job-opportunities coordinator, who will collect and provide the connections and leads for possible employment from church members as well as give support in résumé preparation and job hunting. The church can also provide the directions and support needed to allow George to retrain and retool. Another area of possible assistance could include helping George's wife with baby-sitting assistance and giving her the opportunity to participate in fellowship and study programs. Family and marriage counseling may also fill an important gap.

Along with financial assistance and pastoral support Joan needs enough elbowroom in her life to continue her education and job training. Churches can help provide the necessary support. Many churches minister to so many Joans that they have begun daycare and before-and-after-school programs.

In all these instances churches can network with relatives and with other agencies to provide a substantial amount of help to get people back on their feet. In all these cases the goal should not be to leave people in situations of ongoing dependency but to enable them to become contributing, ministering fellow servants of God.

■ Focus 6: *The Bottom Line*

Ask someone to read Matthew 25:31-46. In closing prayer give praise to God, our provider and sustainer. Ask the group to offer sentence prayers for those who have specific needs in your congregation. Conclude the prayer by thanking God for meeting our needs in so many ways and by praying that in our interdependence we may always recognize our mutual dependence on him.

Options

Option 1: Matching Resources and Needs

Invite a panel to reflect on the ways your church identifies and meets specific needs within the congregation. You might include a deacon, an elder, and a pastor. Or else you may want to invite people with specific needs to reflect on ways in which the church did provide or could have provided support. If you're really brave, try to invite representatives from both of these groups. In that case be prepared to moderate that part of the discussion carefully and sensitively; strong feelings could emerge on both sides. Allow each panel member five to seven minutes to present, and then allow time for input from the class.

Option 2: God Loves a Cheerful Taker

Ask the group to reflect on these questions:

Q. In our Western culture it is much harder to receive than to give. Why?

Various suggestions may be useful here. Undoubtedly, our difficulty with receiving has something to do with our desire to be independent and self-reliant. We somehow equate those qualities with being grown-up and successful.

Q. What can we do to counter that trend so that we encourage those who have need to seek aid and to receive it?

Again, a variety of good suggestions are possible. It would seem that a greater recognition of our interdependence is necessary. We all need help. It's not immaturity that makes it so. That is the way God created us (Gen. 2:18). A stronger emphasis on community and mutual sharing would also help. The real key is probably to show how having people's needs met allows them, in turn, to meet ours. We can accept gifts from others when we, in turn, can contribute them as well.

SESSION ELEVEN

Paul on Pastoral Care (2)

Introductory and Background Comments for the Leader

1 Timothy 5:17-6:2

In our previous session we saw how Paul encourages Timothy to be a good pastor who is sensitive to the different ways in which he must bring the gospel to bear on the varied lives of all God's children. We lingered, as Paul did, on the special care and attention required to minister to the weakest, most vulnerable ones.

Here Paul takes a few sudden leaps. Without warning or apology he jumps from pastoral concerns into three important administrative matters. Then he takes another step, moving from administrative matters to the topic of slavery. For a letter, that is not unusual. Our informal, personal scribbles tend to skip from topic to topic as well.

Earlier Paul had laid down the qualifications for church leaders (1 Tim. 3). Now he deals with issues related to the compensation, discipline, and ordination of leaders. Kooistra calls these "church order matters." A church order is a document that spells out the administrative structure and functions of the church. It can relate to a specific congregation, as in Paul's day, or apply to an entire denomination, as is presently the case in most churches in the Reformed tradition. While such a church order may not offer very stimulating reading, it's very useful. It embodies the vision, aspirations, and values of the community it regulates. As we reflect on Paul's instructions, those three pop into focus.

For example, Paul clearly places a very high value on the ongoing preaching and teaching of God's Word. That is why he argues so strongly for financial compensation for those who do it well. Paul also cares deeply about church leadership. Elders must be protected from slander, or they simply will not dare to function as they should. Conversely, the church must deal forthrightly with legitimate complaints of officebearer misbehavior. It must appropriately and publicly discipline offenders so that members are protected. Justice must done and must also appear to be done. Leaders must be held accountable. They are not exempt from the high standards they inculcate in others. So Paul cautions Timothy to be very careful whom he admits to a leadership position. Time will tell who really possesses the gifts and the trustworthiness to assume leadership. Best not to rush such selections.

Paul interjects some personal advice to Timothy. As he presses Timothy to show concern for church leaders, so Paul himself shows concern for the evangelist. Paul practices what he preaches.

Suddenly Paul takes his next jump. He tackles the complicated issue of slavery. Although in Christ all are free, he deems it wisest for slaves not to upset the applecart. A slave rebellion at this time would severely hinder the spread of the good news. Better to allow the leaven of God's Word to do its work more slowly, to transform the relationships between slaves and their masters into one of full partnership. As Kooistra points out, Paul's advice to slaves drops a time bomb, which will blow apart the social structure with the love of Christ. The old wineskins cannot hold our Savior's new wine without bursting. But the ways of God's kingdom take their time to ripen in our hearts, our lives, and our society.

Purpose of the Study

Our goal in this session will be to explore the values that underlie Paul's instructions: solid preaching and teaching; open, honest, accountable leadership; competent officebearers. Beyond that we will want to see whether those values are worked out sufficiently in our own church. If we can agree that these values still count today, are we convinced that the way our church is set up honors and optimizes them?

We will also want to take a cue from Paul in examining whether we show sufficient concern for our church leaders. Do we give them enough resources, time, and means to do their work well? Do we hold them accountable in a serious, yet loving manner? Do we demonstrate enough concern for their well-being so that they do not burn themselves out? These are issues we want to address. Leadership matters everywhere, including in church.

The topic of showing honor to church leaders sets Paul off in a new direction—whether slaves should also continue to show honor to their masters. Our last goal in this session will be to understand why Paul provides the advice he does on this issue. We will want to give his approach a wider reach as well—to see how it equally applies to other sociological relationships.

■ Focus 1: *Being Careful*

Begin the session by pointing out Paul's sudden transition from pastoral concerns to administrative matters (see Background Comments above). Ask someone to read today's passage, Timothy 5:17-6:2. In prayer, praise God for his greatness and majesty. Praise him as the creator, sustainer, and ruler of the whole universe. Recognize our Lord as the one who alone has been given all authority in heaven and on earth. Thank him for granting gifts of leadership to parents, teachers, church officers, employers, and governors. Pray that God will grant them wisdom, competence, and dedication as they fulfill their responsibilities. May they lead in Jesus' name.

Seek the guidance of God's Spirit in this session so that it will enable you as believers to identify, nurture, activate, and enhance Christ-affirming leadership in your midst.

■ Focus 2: *Paying Pastors*

You may want to lead into the topic by telling this well-traveled anecdote.

At an interdenominational conference three pastors compared the ways in which they received the funds needed to keep body and soul together. The one dressed in patched jeans and a T-shirt said, "I draw a circle on the floor. I throw the entire contents of the Sunday service collection plate into the air. Whatever lands inside the circle is for the Lord. Whatever lands outside the circle is for me."

The preacher dressed in a sports jacket responded that he did things a bit differently: "I draw a line on the floor and heave the Sunday service proceeds into the air; whatever lands on the right side of the line goes to the Lord. What lands on the left side is mine."

The pastor in the fancy tuxedo admitted he used still a different approach: "I take the collection plate and fling its contents into the air; what the Lord wants he keeps. The rest comes down for me."

Observe that preacher compensation is more than just a laughing matter. For many centuries, even before some notable televangelists gave Christianity a black eye by lining their own pockets, preachers have betrayed through their own greed the very gospel they brought. Already in Paul's day many preachers sold Jesus out for the big bucks. This made many believers wonder if it would be wiser not to pay their pastors anything, not because they were cheap but because they wanted to prevent that kind of sellout.

Initiate some discussion by asking the following questions. Jot responses on the board.

Q. Today we see a variety of ways in which evangelists and ministers of the Word receive compensation. What are they?

Some receive none at all. Some receive freewill gifts through offerings. Some must raise their own funds through pledges of support. Others get paid a partial salary while being expected to raise the rest of their income through other employment (tent-maker ministry). Still others give up their own possessions, take a vow of perpetual poverty, and have the church look after their earthly needs. Finally, many get a full salary through their church or agency.

Q. Evaluate these various options. What's good about each? What's bad? In which circumstances would you favor each one?

We should probably resist the temptation to pick one means of support as the one and only appropriate one. While Paul states clearly that preachers/teachers should be paid, he himself will receive only his room and board. He self-funds his ministry by making tents. Under the suspicious gaze of people who have seen too many greedy, selfish preachers, Paul opts for no pay. But he does so by way of exception. He instructs Timothy otherwise: "The worker deserves his wages" (5:18).

Reformation churches have adopted the principle that ministers of the Word should be paid a salary that is sufficient to allow them to devote themselves fully to their calling. However, there are many instances where a minister, an evangelist, or a missionary should continue to serve even though adequate funds are not available. The flock may not be able to raise that kind of money. In those cases a tent-maker type of ministry may be advisable.

Kooistra points out that the system of compensating preachers through freewill offerings is open to abuse. It may also yield funding that is too much or too meager. The general principle should be that preachers get paid steadily and sufficiently enough so that they can carry on their work well. Pay them too much or too little, and finances become too much of a concern for them to do their task well.

■ Focus 3: *Accountable Leaders*

Provide a transition to Paul's next concern by observing that financial considerations alone will not keep preachers on the straight and narrow. There needs to be a healthy accountability structure in the church to supervise the pastor's work as well as that of the elders, deacons, and other church leaders. Paul's concern in verses 19-21 works in two directions: leaders must be shielded from unfair criticism and charges, and at the same time they must be held accountable for their actions.

Provide the class with four copies of the following documents: the church order of your denomination, the bylaws of your congregation, a current church council handbook, and any other documents that relate to the leadership structure of your church. Include not only rules for officebearers but also those relating to Sunday school teachers, worship leaders, and so forth. Divide the class into four groups: those dealing with pastoral staff, elders and deacons, program/ministry leaders, and church education teachers.

Ask each group to examine the policies of your church and to decide whether their assigned church leaders are sufficiently supervised and held accountable in their task(s). Alternatively, if written documentation is really sparse, invite an experienced pastor, elder or deacon, program leader, or church education teacher to meet with the subgroups independently to discuss this question.

Reconvene the groups and have them report on their work. If you identify any weak links, be sure to pass that concern on to your church council. Knowing Paul's concern is not enough. You must decide what your group will do about it.

■ Focus 4: *Trivial Appointments*

Our final trivia battle will deal with the topic of leadership appointments in Scripture. Without further ado, it's time to face the prospective donut buyers with their Waterloo.

Q. What was the name of the "Priest of God Most High" who blessed Abraham?

Melchizedek (Gen. 14:18).

Q. What was the name of at least one of the three Israelites who were swallowed up by the earth because of their challenge to Moses' leadership?

Korah, Dathan, and Abiram (Num. 16:1).

Q. What sign did Elisha receive to convince him that he had been equipped and chosen by God to take up Elijah's prophetic task?

He witnessed Elijah being taken away from him in a chariot of fire.

Q. What do the words "Messiah" and "Christ" mean?

Anointed One.

Q. Through the leaders of which church did God appoint Paul as an apostle to the gentiles?

Antioch (Acts 13:1-3).

Q. In the life-to-come, believers will be given authority to judge the world and a certain group of beings as well. What group?

Angels (1 Cor. 6:3).

The time of reckoning has come. The cumulative score tells the story. The losing team has to provide donuts at the next session, and that's all there is to it. You will have to endure some bragging and recriminations, but fair's fair. If the score is tied, all the better: both teams bring donuts.

■ Focus 5: *Taking Care*

You might want to wonder out loud: would Paul approve of your class gobbling down donuts while poring over his personal letters? He certainly does not seem to have any problem advising Timothy to drink some wine while absorbing his advice. He shows genuine concern for the evangelist's well-being. We need to show that kind of concern for our leaders as well. In light of that idea, discuss the following question.

Q. What care should your church give its leaders to enable them to do their work well? Does your church provide it?

Jot the group's suggestions on the board in a vertical column. Be sure to include the following items if they are not forthcoming:

- prayer
- a clear task description
- appropriate training and ongoing education
- encouragement
- cooperation
- honest, loving feedback
- a clear, functioning accountability structure
- official backup and support for difficult decisions
- loving, humble admonition
- teamwork
- a peer consultation process
- adequate financial compensation for paid staff
- adequate time for replenishment and rest
- a graceful exit to other ministry possibilities

Run the various leadership positions through this grid and see if the group can spot any areas that need work. If you identify any, what will your class do about it? We need to remind ourselves that gaining and keeping healthy church leadership is every member's business.

■ Focus 6: *Slaves Who Bide God's Time*

At this point in the lesson confess that you have no clue how you can tie Paul's last point, about slaves, into the previous discussion. But you should deal with it nevertheless, so here goes.

Quote Kooistra's comment that 6:1-2 "places a time bomb under the institution of slavery." Once masters and slaves see each other as brothers, the idea of slavery becomes uncomfortable to both of them and ultimately dissolves into partnership.

Q. Does that wisdom apply to other forms of social inequity as well? Which ones? How?

Besides slaves Kooistra mentions women and people of different ethnic backgrounds, religions, or sexual orientations. In all these cases we cannot simply overturn the applecart in one swoop. We'll have to keep plugging away at the good old news that in Christ we may all find perfect unity. Only that gospel can, and will, erode the horrible inequities that tear us apart—rich and poor, male and female, black and white, gentile and Jew.

■ Focus 7: *In Closing*

Ask your group to spend a few moments reflecting on the misery caused in this world by social injustices that keep us apart and enslaved. End with sentence prayers for those who feel the deep sting of having their freedom and joy in Christ compromised by others. Pray that your church may be a healing force in your community and in the world.

Remind the trivia-trounced that they have some homework they need to bring to the next session and that some of it had better have chocolate on it.

Options

Option 1: Comparing Bank Notes

Invite a missionary or pastor who lives only from donations, as well as one who receives a full salary, to meet with you. Ask them for their reflections on the pluses and minuses of making their living in the way that they do.

Option 2: Putting Pastors to Work

Challenge the class to develop an appropriate job description for your senior pastor. Use the board and work as a committee of the whole. For headings put down TASKS, HOURS SPENT, and ACCOUNTABILITY. Once your group has run out of jobs to keep the pastor occupied, ask them to rate these tasks in order of priority. Does the job description appear workable? Would you take the job under those conditions?

Option 3: Advising Slaves

Ask someone to read to the class Paul's letter to Philemon. Ask participants individually to spend some time writing a similar letter that Paul might have written to Onesimus. Share results.

SESSION TWELVE

Timothy's Treasure

Introductory and Background Comments for the Leader

1 Timothy 6:3-21

In our last session we explored how Paul's concern for good leadership in the church carries over into the present. A lot has changed since Paul's time. But leadership still matters as much today as it did in his day, maybe more. Providing resources for leaders, structuring proper accountability, and showing concern for our leaders' own, personal well-being are all matters that still occupy us today.

It would be marvelous if Paul's appended comments about slavery would no longer be relevant today. We could drop any discussion of it. But as we saw last time, that is not the case. Slavery still exists in many forms in our world. So do other, equally destructive social forces by which we rob each other of our freedom in Christ. The reach of the gospel still has far to go before our cruel inequalities will dissolve fully into loving fellowship.

In this last session we will once more flit from topic to topic, following the twists and turns of Paul's parting thoughts. Paul takes one final swipe at false teachers. He exposes them as ignorant people who provoke useless arguments for their own financial gain. As Kooistra puts it, "Jesus' words heal, theirs make you sick." False teaching is one of the two things that Paul warns Timothy to strenuously avoid: "But you, man of God, flee from all this" (v. 11).

The other thing Timothy must avoid is the pursuit of wealth. While riches and earthly goods are gifts of God, undue concern and desire for them are not: "The love of money is a root of all kinds of evil" (v. 10). How easily preachers and leaders fall into the trap of selling out the gospel. They use it to squeeze out a healthy pile of money for themselves. Too late they find out that when the trap snaps shut, their credibility is blown sky-high. They "have wandered from the faith and pierced themselves with many griefs" (v. 10). That slippery slope, too, Timothy must strenuously avoid.

Warning Timothy away from chasing such things, Paul tells him what he *should* pursue and for what he *should* fight. Timothy should "pursue righteousness, godliness, faith, love, endurance and gentleness (v. 11). He should "fight the good fight of the faith" and "take hold of . . . eternal life" (v. 12). To emphasize the full seriousness of this command, Paul turns it into a formal charge to the evangelist. He solemnly invokes God's name and ends this bottom-line injunction with a doxology. He raises a beautiful hymn of praise to the one who alone can turn our hope into reality when our Lord returns. That hope will keep Timothy on track.

In verses 17-21 Paul plays one last variation on the two themes with which he began this section: wealth and heresy. He instructs Timothy to command rich believers to put their faith in God, not in their wealth. And he says they should be generous in sharing it. With his final instruction Paul ends where he started both this section and his entire letter. His prime concern is that Timothy and his flock remain firmly in the true faith, avoiding the pitfalls of false teaching and fake knowledge.

Paul closes 1 Timothy with a very brief "Grace be with you." Kooistra points out that in the Greek the *you* is in the plural. While Timothy is his prime reader, Paul realizes that Timothy will share this letter with his fellow believers. Beyond them, over thousands of years, his sound instruction and benediction still fall firmly and sweetly on our ears as well.

The repetition of topics we find in this passage gives you, as leader, the opportunity to provide some closure to this course. It will give you the chance to review what we have learned along the way. It will also allow you to revisit any questions that were left unanswered. You may want to invite someone who can help you sort out the thorny, recurring ones to join your class for this last session. As you revisit some of

Paul's recurring themes, you will want to highlight those features of the passage that contribute something new to them.

Kooistra appropriately ends with Paul's marvelous doxology (vv. 15-16). Similarly, you may want to end the session and the course with a time of worship. Prayer, singing, and a time of reflection in which participants share what they have learned can all be excellent ways to part company.

Purpose of the Study

Your main goal today will be to review the larger themes that Paul revisits in this closing passage. In the process you will want to allow your class to sense the urgency and richness with which Paul presents the bottom line one last time. His plea to Timothy to "fight the good fight of the faith" (v. 12) undergirds this whole passage. The timid evangelist must single-mindedly pursue his mission to bring the truth of God's Word to his flock—the whole truth and nothing but the truth. He must do it with purity of heart without getting diverted by worldly concerns and pursuits.

This bottom line must also impact our lives. God invites us along on his mission. Maybe God does not call us to be apostles or evangelists, but he does direct his call to us as believers. How committed to it are we? Do we know what it is? Our real purpose in this final session is to leave each participant with those crucial questions.

■ Focus 1: *Beginning to Conclude*

Summarize the agenda for this session by telling the class that Paul's concluding passage reminds us of what we should *not* do. Then it emphatically tells us what we *should* do. While Paul does not speak these words directly to us, his closing "Grace be with you [plural in Greek]" indicates that he was targeting his straight talk to others as well. He looks over Timothy's shoulder at the saints in Ephesus and beyond them at all believers, us included. Having challenged us to "fight the good fight of the faith" (v. 12), he leaves us in the care of the one who alone can give us the grace to do it. As he does so, Paul takes his leave with a marvelous doxology. We will follow Kooistra's lead by ending our session celebrating it, not dissecting it.

Invite someone to read 1 Timothy 6:3-21. In prayer seek God's direction as you try to sort out what Paul's challenge means to each one of us. Ask that God's Spirit may open our minds to see our mission and give us the strength of faith to pursue it with all our hearts.

■ Focus 2: *What to Chase*

Ask the class to respond to these questions.

Q. Is false doctrine a danger in your life? How?

Participants might come up with some startling answers to this question. Take enough time to reflect on them if they do. More likely, your group will not be able to think of a specific example, so you may have to prime the pump a little. In session 3 we learned that false teaching does not only come in the guise of outright denials of our beliefs. It does not just come knocking at our door carrying a pamphlet or magazine. It constantly filters into our homes through media messages and modern patterns of thought. We often simply adopt those patterns without thinking them through: "Everybody's beliefs are as good as mine"; "We all believe in the same God"; "When you have your health, you have everything."

Allow some time for the group to share responses, then press on with the next question.

Q. Describe what Paul means by "godliness with contentment" (v. 6). Is that hard to achieve for you?

To answer this question, you can refer back to Kooistra's discussion in chapters 4, 9, and 12. "Godliness" describes a life lived in a vibrant, healthy relationship with God. Here it refers to the genuine desire to live that kind of life. "Contentment" in this context means that we are self-sufficient, not needing anything more than the basics because we find our treasure in Christ. Satisfied with the basics of life, we have learned to give up the trivial pursuit of earthly gain in favor of striving for true godliness. That's easier said than done in a world that spends billions on convincing us we need more of every imaginable product that's for sale. Spend some time discussing how class members and their families struggle with this.

Q. By biblical standards people who have anything more than roofs over their heads and food in their stomachs are wealthy. Is it wrong for us to have more than the basics?

Paul makes it clear in verses 17-19 that having wealth is not a problem as long as two considerations apply. The first is that wealthy people must recognize that their riches will not save them and that, just like the poor, they must place their hope in God. Secondly, wealthy people must be generous with their riches, willingly sharing with those in need.

■ Focus 3: *A Serious Charge*

Observe that Paul has arrived at the bottom line. In verses 11 and 12 he reminds Timothy one last time of what he should pursue, for what he should fight, of what he should take hold. We sense how densely Paul packs and compresses these verses with all his urgent, passionate desire for the young evangelist to serve boldly and wholeheartedly as a soldier of the cross.

Divide the class into groups of two or three and ask them to share what some of these terms in verses 11 and 12 might mean for their own lives. They do not need to write anything down or to report back to the group on their conversations. This is their opportunity to look for concrete connections they can make between these crucial objectives and their own lives.

After you reconvene the class, allow some time for questions or comments arising out of their conversations.

■ Focus 4: *Trivial Review*

The time has come to share the bounteous booty. To the victors go the spoils and to the vanquished as well—*if* there are enough donuts to go around, that is. But not so fast! Participants will have to work for their prize.

Ask everyone to make up two trivia questions based on 1 Timothy and write them on a slip of paper. Collect the questions and ask them one at a time. Obviously the person writing the question should not answer it, but it's fair game for everyone else. The first person to answer the question correctly gets to pick a donut and may chomp away. If no one knows the correct answer, then the person who wrote the question gets the donut. Those who have a donut are out for the duration of the game because there is an ancient rule against answering trivia questions with your mouth full. Should the group be unable to answer a question posed by someone who is already dismembering an apple fritter, just go on to the next question. If you run out of questions, deal out the remaining donuts and call it a day.

■ Focus 5: *Do You Hear God's Call?*

Allow some time for small talk. Then refocus the group by asking participants to sharpen their pencils one last time. Have them reread for themselves Paul's charge to Timothy in verses 12-15a. Ask them to write down what they see as their God-given mission. What concretely should they do in their lives to fulfil God's call to them? Timothy's task was to preach and teach the Gospel. What's theirs?

After they have had a chance to think about that and complete their answers, ask if anyone would like to share his/her response, but don't prompt anyone to do so. Suggest that what they have written may be useful for them to look at during closing devotions.

■ **Focus 6: *Grace Be With You***

Take the opportunity to thank class members for their participation, their input, and their contributions. Make any other comments or announcements you wish to make and then invite the class to join you in closing worship. Paul's words in verses 15b-16 offer a fitting conclusion to this course. Invite someone to read them aloud to the class. You may want to include a fresh, relevant devotional that is pertinent to this passage or theme as well. Spend some time singing songs of praise that you have selected and if need be invite a qualified song leader and/or accompanist to assist you.

Close the session in prayer. Invite sentence prayers that continue to direct our praise and thanks to God. You may wish to conclude the prayer, asking God to make his call clear to each one. Pray that God will equip, motivate, and guide us to remain firm in our faith as we fight the good fight. After urging participants to recommit themselves to their task and calling, allow some time for silent prayer. Conclude the prayer with a suitable parting song of praise.

Options

Option 1: Always Content

Ask someone to read Philippians 4:11-13, and then ask group members if they believe it is possible to be content in every situation. Have they seen examples of people who have this attitude? Allow them to swap some stories on this point.

Option 2: In Summary

Take some time to stand back a bit and look at the forest instead of the individual trees. Ask participants to reread 1 Timothy and to jot down in fifty words or less what its main theme is. Then ask them to write down what they found to be the most surprising, interesting, or inspiring feature about this letter. Share responses.

Option 3: Taking Stock

As your group reflected on 1 Timothy, a number of issues emerged that would provide some helpful suggestions to your church leadership on how better to flesh out the vision that Paul has for the church. This may be a good opportunity to entertain some feedback on how those suggestions were received. Did any changes result?